SICILY

Land of Love and Strife

A FILMMAKER'S JOURNEY

To Audrey
Love
Mark

SICILY

Land of Love and Strife

A FILMMAKER'S JOURNEY

Mark Spano

Sicily: Land of Love and Strife
A Filmmaker's Journey
Mark Spano

Published by Thunderfoot Press
2018

Portions of this book have appeared in slightly different form in The Times of Sicily in both print and online publications.
www.timesofsicily.com

Note: For the sake of consistency and in fairness to those living who expressed a desire not to be mentioned by name in these pages and those dead who were unable to express a preference, I have fictionalized some of the names of persons save historical figures and my own.

MKS, 2018, Chapel Hill, NC, USA
Published by
Thunderfoot Press
Chapel Hill, North Carolina, U.S.A.
www.thunderpress.com
www.sicilymovie.com
ISBN: 13: 978-0-9976027-1-5
Library of Congress Control Number: 2018909510

Artwork provided by DreamScape Media LLC
Book design by Jeff Crawford

In Memory of Floyd Buhler

FORWARD

by Karen La Rosa, Sicily aficionada

Karen La Rosa

Stories, photos, and letters from bygone generations engage the imagination and create images of our family that we cherish. They represent our lineage, the place from which we came. Dreams. Pictures of dour faces, long dresses, and mustaches, faded papers filled with ornately cursive, almost illegible letters, all remind of us of the lives of our ancestors. When enough curiosity mounts and the right moment comes along, we may decide to visit our ancestral homeland. What we will find is something the imagination cannot provide. Breathing the same air and walking the same streets, when you take that soil in your hands and drink from the same fountain that our family did so many years ago. A connection is made that is much stronger than what can be imagined. You come closer to who they were and to their reality by immersing ourselves in their experiences.

Mark Spano's family left Sicily and landed in Kansas City with many other families from the center of Palermo. He was fascinated by the history and when his moment came, off to Sicily he went.

What a journey ensued. Over the course of many visits, Mark's observations and encounters led him to a clearer understanding of his personal history and that of Sicily as a whole, yet he found more questions.

A writer and filmmaker is always asking questions and his documentary "Sicily: Land of Love and Strife" is the answer to some of his. During Mark's time on the island and during the week we spent together, Mark interviewed a wide variety of people from the Mayor of Palermo to a local baker, from a rap singer to a tour guide, more material than he could fit into the film, but he finally arrived at the place where he felt ready to share his interpretations.

To his own eye, a broader picture of Sicily's history, its complicated issues, and unique evolution, presented itself. Good film editing brought it all to life and the result is a compelling feature-length documentary. This companion book gives the reader the personal background—an inkling into Mark's point of view. It engages the reader and enables a better understanding of his journey both as a child in a Sicilian neighborhood in Kansas City and as an adult walking the narrow lanes of the Vucciria in Palermo.

Mark and I connected because we had both delved deeply into the mystery that is Sicily. From early years, my Sicilian heritage captivated my attentions. When my time was right, I went there and subsequently started a business to share my love of the island. with tourists.

In our own ways, we have both tried to capture the elusive, as, over time, so many before us have done. Yet to describe the indescribable is impossible. To state an authoritative conclusion about a place with such a complex and varied past is also impossible. In the end, all we can do is add our own perspectives to the compendia of others and hope that the curious will find a well-rounded depiction.

Mark has generously shared a very personal and unique view of Sicily in the direction of his terrific documentary. This intriguing companion book, which peeks inside its author, will bring you along on his continuing Sicilian odyssey—his quest to understand and describe the island that is Sicily.

ACKNOWLEDGEMENTS

I wish to thank my best friend and life-partner Carlus Walters for his understanding and patience during the time I was writing this book. I also wish to thank my friend and colleague Kim Weiss for her invaluable editorial advice.

MKS, 2018, Chapel Hill, NC, USA

❝...the truth about anything is nobody's monopoly—
not least, the truth about a place. **❞**
—Jan Morris

*Left: The author's Paternal grand-
parents, Angelo Spano & Oliva
Inzerillo Spano*

*Below: The author's parents,
Frank Spano & Helen Pellegrino
Spano*

The Spano children: Susan, Ronald & the author

ONE

I grew up in a blue-collar, downtown neighborhood halfway
between Kansas City's North End and Northeast. The
North End, near the City Market, was where many Sicilians
and Neapolitans settled in the late nineteenth and early
twentieth centuries. My father's people settled first in the
North End, and my father was born there.

The Northeast was a leafy neighborhood of boulevards,
where many of those very first Sicilian and Neapolitan
arrivals matriculated when they had taken some steps up the
great American socio-economic ladder. My mother's family
lived in the Northeast, and my mother was born there.

The Northeast and the North End were not all that distant
from each other. This was key. If there was a step-up that
could be taken by Sicilians and other southern Italians, that
step had to be taken within the sight of those left behind, or
else there would be no point. For these people, for my people,
change was not change, progress was not progress unless it

was visible. What benefit would there be to have made good, if the less fortunate of your community could not witness your prosperity? Secret prosperity was meaningless.

The Great Depression hit both my parents' families hard. My father's family fell apart. My mother's relatives were better prepared emotionally and financially and weathered the worst of the Depression years. In 1933, my mother's best friend had a cousin who was tall and good-looking. Wouldn't my sixteen-year-old, yet-to-be mother like to have her friend's handsome cousin (my yet-to-be father) take her to the prom?

Of course, she did. It was love at first sight. But my father had no job and little prospect of one. My mother's father was dead set against it. And, anyway, the boy was unemployed, from the North End, and most inauspiciously, he was Sicilian.

My maternal grandfather was from a tiny and extremely poor village in Apulia. It seems the men from this village took religion much more seriously than most Sicilian men. My mother's relatives were more resolute and upright than my father's. A couple of my paternal uncles ended up in the local newspapers when they were arrested for petty crimes.

My mother's father believed no good would come of the match between his daughter and the tall, handsome Sicilian. Despite Grandpa's objections, my parents dated until 1942, when my father enlisted in the army so he would have enough money to marry my mother. My parents were married a few months before he was sent overseas.

My sister was born while my father was overseas. So after the war, they moved to the neighborhood where I was born and raised. We lived in a tiny flat in a mixed industrial and residential neighborhood between the North End and the Northeast. It had been Irish, but by the late 1940s, the Irish had all but disappeared. Some Sicilians and other southern Italians remained, as well as smaller ethnic cadres from

Mexico and eastern Europe, and even a few Syrians and Lebanese.

By age fourteen, most of us knew who among our neighbors were criminals and who were not. A fact of life. We were street kids, noisy and bored. Most of us were Catholics. There was crime in our neighborhood, but we didn't consider gambling as criminal, even though it was illegal when I was a boy. Stupid maybe, but not criminal.

We knew crime. Crime was drugs, guns, prostitution, "protection" and the sale of stolen goods. It was everywhere. We saw it at a very early age and knew exactly what we were seeing. We also knew exactly what our parents thought about it, and more importantly what was expected of us in the face of it. A criminal life was unthinkable in my family. That was that. My family, like many Sicilians and southern Italians, may have been overly sensitive about what others might think about this or that turn of events, but they were honest to a fault and had no use for the allure of easy money that so captivated some of our neighbors.

My father worked in a steel mill. Until we had a car, which was not until 1955, he took the bus to a hot, noisy and miserable job. I was the youngest of three children. When I started first grade my mother went to work as a bookkeeper for a mail order company.

At fourteen I was accepted to the Jesuit boys' prep school clear across town. The tuition was $300 a year. In 1964, this was a considerable sum for my family. It was supposedly the best school I could attend. More to the point, it was the best Catholic school I could attend. So, there I was every morning, twenty miles across town, a greaser among the preppies.

Within days of my arrival at that school, I was approached by a classmate who lived across town where my school was. I will call him Jimmy Santangelo. He was a Sicilian kid but dressed very preppy. I knew some of his relations who lived near me. The first thing he said to me was, "Hey, Spanò, you come from the North Side. Your Dad must be in the Mafia."

I knew Santangelo's family. His grandfather had been the biggest bootlegger in our town. But like gambling, I never considered bootlegging much of a crime. Lots of people had done it during Prohibition. So what? Turns out, Santangelo's granddad provided not only bathtub gin that made many a drinker go blind. Nonnu Santangelo also delivered the muscle to protect his operation and the operations of his pals across town. Nonnu Santangelo was a mean, violent man and he killed lots of people. He shot a distant relative of mine, about age ten, off a produce huckster's truck to prove some kind of point. I knew this. Everyone, where I grew up, knew this. Jimmy Santangelo, though, did not know it. I certainly wasn't going to tell him that he lived across town because his grandfather had been a bootlegger and a murderer.

It was, though, from that comment by the young and sadly uninformed Santangelo that I began to notice that the world only knew one thing about Sicilians, and that was crime. Even Sicilians themselves like Santangelo displaced their erroneous notions about Sicilians on others. It was a financial challenge for my family to send me to that school. But because I had a Sicilian background and came from the old neighborhood, I must be a gangster's kid.

I came from a family of readers, and at one point in my life, I began to read about Sicily. I learned there was crime in Sicily like in the neighborhood of my childhood, that was undeniable. But I also learned there was so much more to Sicily, to being Sicilian, that I could not imagine why the entire planet had fallen for such a cheap ruse.

Most John Wayne fans are surprised to find out that a great many cowboys from the Old West were black men, because we learned most of what we thought we knew about American cowboys from the movies. That depiction has little or nothing to do with what actually happened in the authentic history of the American West.

Sicilians have also had their American stories told by filmmakers. And let's face it, shoot'em-up criminals make for a more exciting film than men working union jobs, living in substandard housing, and raising three children by the skin of their teeth. I love gangster movies as a genre. They can be great entertainment. But their content, no matter how well-crafted, is fiction having little or nothing to do with the people who lived for more than three thousand years on a triangular-shaped island at the toe of the Italian peninsula.

This story is my attempt to find a Sicily that is not fictitious. A Sicily that tells me more about myself than gangster movies. This is not everyone's story of Sicily. It is mine. It is a record of where my reading and travels have taken me.

The biochemist Rupert Sheldrake coined the term "morphic resonance," which is "the idea that, through a telepathic effect or sympathetic vibration, an event or act can lead to similar events or acts in the future; or an idea conceived in one mind can then arise in another."

There is, as you might imagine, some disagreement whether this is a valid scientific concept. But for the sake of a reasonably useful conceptual tool, I am going to assume that Dr. Sheldrake is correct.

What is Sicily? What has happened in Sicily? How have events over the last three thousand years resonated in the lives and personalities of the island's people? How have the people from this island influenced events, ideas, and tastes across our planet? And, how has this island where I have never lived, where my father never lived, a place where grandparents and great aunts and uncles were born and departed, how has this island influenced me?

Are my feelings of "Sicilian-ness" simply imaginative constructions? Or, does Sicily, its people, its stories, and its terrain have considerable sway on who I am and what I have become?

Despite my father's sketchy education and hard-knocks upbringing, he was an avid and voluminous reader. These factors likely contributed markedly to his characteristic Sicilian cynicism. He did not view history, religion, or macroeconomics as somehow flawed. Rather, he saw them as skillfully thought-out and finely articulated areas of inquiry that were utterly and quite intentionally deceptive. My father was capable of rigorous and compelling denial of even the slightest good intention in relation to most of the world's scholarship. When I was young I vehemently disagreed with my father's worldview that most global institutions were colluding in some mass economic conspiracy. In midlife I found his ideas to be part of the comedy we attribute to the families we grew away from because of our travels, education, and careers.

My father masterfully articulated his ideas, punctuating his orations with the occasional f-bomb to my mother's unflagging disapproval. Such words should not be spoken in the presence of her grandchildren. These discussions were always fun in sort of a mean-spirited way. This upbraiding of the whole world was something for my siblings and me to enjoy. It was part of our family's oral history. It remains for us a vivid memory.

In the latter third of my life, I am beginning to understand that my father's observations were not entirely incorrect. The deck is stacked everywhere. Sicily, so often subjected to external forces and lacking control of its own destiny, has been a poster child my father's idée fixe, of history as a stacked deck.

My credentials as the author of a book and the writer/producer/director of a film about Sicily are simultaneously extensive and meager. My reading has been extensive. But I did not visit Sicily for the first time until I was sixty years old. My Italian is rudimentary at best. I have yet to find blood relatives in Sicily. But I am drawn there like a pilgrim to Mecca. As I sit at my keyboard in the office of my North Carolina home, I wish only to be in Sicily. My nose itches for the smells of Persephone's Island.

And, what if anything, does any of this have to do with the Kansas City of my upbringing in the 1950s and '60s? This book and the film are attempts to find connections among the threads of my adult life, the inner city life of my childhood and the mysterious land of my grandparents.

Through all of the stories and lore of my family, I was told of a Sicily that never truly existed for me. I am not altogether certain that it existed for my relatives in the ways they described it. It is a place that in this writing I am reimagining. This story of Sicily will embody the ebb and flow of these varied and remarkable occurrences through the pre-Socratic Sicilian Philosopher Empedocles' prism of Love and Strife.

This book and the film recount my meetings with Sicilians in the places where my forebears worked, played, prayed, loved, and struggled. By witnessing how Sicilians live their lives today, I will bring to life a fuller picture of the great dichotomy that is Sicily.

Above: The Church of San Domenico

La Zisa

Palazzina Cinese

TWO

Quannu en Sicilia fate commu uno Siciliano.
[When in Sicily act like a Sicilian.]

—A Sicilian Proverb

At the very toe of the boot-shaped Italian peninsula, there, surrounded by seas, sits a rocky, three-sided island that has been called Sikelia, Magna Graecia, Thrinacia, Trinacria, Triquerta, Siquillia and Persephone's Island. This is a place once inhabited by the ancient tribes of Sicani, Sicels, and Elymians. Ownership of this rugged and fertile terrain has been contested for nearly as long as historical memory. Because of the island's great natural abundance and its strategic location in the Mediterranean, it has been fought over by Greeks, North African Muslims, Phoenicians, Romans, Ostrogoths, Vandals, Byzantines, Arabs, Normans, Lombards, English, Aragonese, Spanish, Austrians, Italians, Germans, Canadians and Americans. My Sicilian family is a product of this history of invasion and conquest, although few of them, if any, were aware of it.

My father's people were fruit and vegetable vendors in the Vucciria market in Palermo. Upon arriving in the United States, most of them engaged in this same work in the City Market of Kansas City, Missouri.

Through ancient times and into the Twentieth Century, there were continual struggles to control their island homeland. A number of languages were and still are spoken there, including Greek, Arabic, Latin, Hebrew, French, Spanish, Catalan, Albanian, Italian and a wide variety of local dialects. My grandparents spoke a Palermo dialect.

Languages, cultures, and religions confronted one another on Sicily, often, with cruel consequences. This confluence of forces brought about a place and culture that blends Europe, Africa, and the Middle East; it is all of them and yet none of them. This place's uniquely alloyed culture has touched most of the planet with its art, architecture, literature, philosophy, economics, history, food and agriculture.

The pre-Socratic Sicilian philosopher Empedocles believed that love was the earthly force that brought things together and strife the force that pulled things apart. The Sicily from which my progenitors hailed gave them the love and strife of Empedocles, the strife being so all-pervasive that they were able to experience very little of the diverse cultures that had evolved in Sicily.

I stand at the Palace La Zisa with Norman, Muslim, Roman and Byzantine stylistic influences infused throughout the structure. My reading tells me it is one of the most important architectural remnants in Palermo. I am awed by a singular mosaic of archers, peacocks, and palms in this palace, which dates to 900 CE. I wonder if my grandmother ever saw it. It was just a couple of miles across the city from where she lived. She probably did not even know of its existence or that Norman conquerors used Moorish supervisors to design and build their architectural monuments.

Palazzina Cinese, the most unusual edifice I have ever seen in my life, is a hunting lodge that the Bourbons constructed at the edge of La Favorita, once a giant royal hunting ground on the outskirts of Palermo that is now a park famous for its magnificent palm trees. Palazzina Cinese is exquisitely Sicilian. It is decoratively painted inside and out in elaborate, early Nineteenth Century chinoiserie. Floor to ceiling, everything is covered with either extremely stylized Chinese scenes or geometric orientalism. The colors are the vibrant and primary hues of the Sicilian coast. My eyes almost refuse to believe the products of the combined efforts of the Sicilian sun and these saturated colors.

If some works of Sicilian art and architecture are over the top, Palazzina Cinese is the most over the top. It is a building as idiosyncratic as an opera. The excesses of Richard Strauss's Der Rosenkavalier come to mind. Some critics say they cannot abide such excess. But much of what is excessive in the world—that which tastemakers like to call crass—is well-loved by ordinary people. I for one, genuinely revere the Palazzina Cinese.

Through the trees of La Favorita, I photograph the exterior of the Palazzina; I think my grandfather may have walked through this park. He might have seen the very views and angles of the building I am shooting. Did he ever go inside? I want to believe he did.

Carlus and I play chicken up-close and personal walking into oncoming Palermo traffic, passing under the narrow entrance of the Porta Nuova. Certainly, one or both of my grandparents, a great uncle, great aunt, or cousin had to have passed under this same gate coming into or leaving Palermo.

I frequently catch myself wondering about what I cannot possibly know and likely will never learn. So much about this place evokes in me an eerie curiosity. Why do I care so much? What the devil am I searching for? Not yet certain what and why I seek, I continue to explore.

Spaniards, Greeks, Italians, Normans, Arabs, and

Jews all lived in close proximity to one another in Palermo, each group endeavoring to maintain their own customs and traditions. Sicilians like my grandparents likely experienced little of these nearby, "foreign" strangers. Ethnic intermingling is a modern notion. Family members may have lived close to peoples very different from themselves, but from all I glean from reading and talking to Sicilians, intermingling was almost unimaginable.

So, in Sicily my father's family had little opportunity to find out about other tribes. Emigration changed that.

In Sicily, they lived outside of the mainstream of 19th century Europe and emigrated to a 20th century United States, their exposure to the diversity of the New World was immediate. It must have been bewildering to have been pitched into the deep end of the pool of work and business for people who had been so sheltered by family and so deprived of useful knowledge by religion. My father's people were lost in emigration.

This is my story of the place from which my father's people came. It is of a place and people that I discovered in my own personal fashion. My paternal relatives did not fare all that well in the New World. My father's parents and most of his many siblings were not big winners in the great American lottery of economic mobility. They were as good as any other people, but they were naïve, unprepared for the American challenge.

As I piece together the few fragments of information I have about them as a group or individually, I believe Sicily was as perplexing to them as the New World. They were simply unprepared for what America held in store.

The Sicilians of my Kansas City childhood and Sicilians in Sicily have very distinctive noses, some aquiline, some bridged with a crook right at center-face, some rounder than they are long. Il naso is often the most prominent facial feature, competing only with the eyes for top billing on the Sicilian visage.

Noses in Sicily are extremely important. I believe my own strongest sense of awareness is olfactory. I have a Sicilian nose in terms of its size and shape, and it is a major apparatus for understanding my environment.

We Sicilians do possess a strong sense of the visual, but my greatest insights come to me via my nostrils. The sense of smell has diminished in most homo sapiens over the millennia but not so much for me. Even though I am two generations away from that three-sided island, I believe (but certainly cannot prove) my Sicilian DNA has endowed me with knowledge of the world that is achievable only through smells.

On my first walk through the Vucciria, Palermo's old open-air marketplace, I feel as if I'm in someplace familiar though I have never walked those streets before in my life and have heard very little about the place. I am sure it's the smells.

My innkeeper Giuseppe tells me that Vucciria is a market in decline. I should go to the Capo or Ballarò instead. No, I can't, I tell him. Vucciria is the market where my father's family worked. They left the produce business of Vucciria in Palermo and moved to the produce business in the City Market of Kansas City, Missouri.

Vucciria is located at the foot of the church of San Domenico. There are some cafes around the piazza. Down the steep and narrow side-streets, the market begins. Every manner of antiquity is represented in Sicily. Some places are old, worn and venerable. Vucciria is not that. The stones of the streets and buildings of this market are old from overuse. They are old from layer upon layer of tire rubber, produce, meat, and fish grime underfoot. Old from paint and placards slapped one upon another dating back to when? No one knows.

This is not one of the spruced-up, revered European markets

the likes of Rue Cler or La Boqueria St. Joseph. Vucciria is stall upon stall squeezed into almost no space. The proximity of surrounding buildings shades the market for most of the day, the congested passages nearly without sunlight in one of the sunniest places on the planet. Cars, trucks, and motorbikes move in and out freely among the pedestrians.

And there is noise. In Sicily, there is noise almost everywhere. Nothing is quiet in Sicily. The vehicles rattle and puff, brakes squeak, gears grind, and Vespas sputter like flatulent old men. Everyone is yelling, yelling to sell, yelling to complain, yelling to say hello, yelling to curse an enemy, or yelling to profess undying love to the shapely dark-eyed madonna doing her morning shopping.

And the smells. In the piazza of San Domenico there is the blended funk of exhaust, horse piss, last night's mussels and clams with white wine and garlic and stale beer. On the first steps down the shady corridors of the market itself, there is the stench of bloody pork innards and overripe apricots. An old man, skinny and gnarled with more grey hair on his ears than on his reddened and scaly head, turns sausages on a makeshift charcoal grill in front of a stall. My eyes burn from the smoke as do his. A neighboring vendor woman complains to him of the smoke. The crusty man chuckles a little and continues turning his links.

As I walk the market, breads, burnt sugar, butter, citrus, and coffee combine in a single morning smell that makes me want to fall asleep. I am not sleepy long, however, jolted by the olfactory assaults of the fish stalls. Some odors can only make one more alert. The fishmongers are happy men, young and old, good-naturedly insulting one another as they work, sharpening knives, and gutting the day's catch with a minimum of blade movement.

There are flowers and produce of every variety in the

market. Trinkets, blankets and designer knock-offs. Women and girls walk the market. The boys and men stand around. All males stand around in Sicily. They pose and preen. They smoke cigarettes and roll their sleeves. They gaze with seeming disinterest in all that passes.

Many of the vendors are not native Sicilians. There are Indians and Pakistanis, Koreans, Chinese, and Indonesians. Hearing people with East Asian accents speak Italian has always struck me as strange. I'm not sure why. At the Palermo airport, I once heard a taxi driver whom I guessed to be of Korean origin cursing a colleague in the crowd of massed taxis in the airport drive-up. Hearing this man with his East Asian appearance using the Sicilian vulgarities and anatomical curses of my Kansas City childhood seemed absurd. It reminded me of the time I saw a Tibetan monk wrapped snugly in his red robes transacting business at an ATM in Greensboro, North Carolina—something that also made me laugh for reasons I do not completely comprehend.

I walk Vucciria again and again. I never tire of it.

Our innkeeper Giuseppe is a man of indeterminate age. He may be as young as his late fifties or as old as seventy-five. He is up very early. He is surprised to find me in the sunroom reading at 6 a.m. He apologizes profusely because I have no coffee. "Tomorrow morning, I will have coffee for you by six."

"That's not necessary," I reply. "I'm fine."

The next morning, I was in the sunroom a little before six. A thermal carafe of freshly brewed coffee is waiting for me on the sideboard.

Giuseppe is a Palermitan. We are staying at the downtown palazzo of his mother's family, which he converted to a guest house with a subsidy from the European Union. He refinished the terrazzo floors himself, and they are breathtaking. I had thought that they are original to this downtown Baroque building, where Carlus and I were staying on our first visit to Sicily.

Carlus and the rest of the guests at Giuseppe's Palazzo are still sleeping. With coffee and an unopened notebook and pen, the morning sun is a time of meditation for me. "Please world," I whisper into my cup, "leave me alone this morning."

Every journal entry or poem I've ever written in the early morning is either a salutation to the quiet joy of having morning to myself or a grunt of utter contempt for whatever job I'm working that has robbed me of the quiet joy of owning the morning. Whether I produce any worthwhile notes or writing this morning is neither here nor there. My body wants its morning. It wants its morning alone.

On this particular morning, I need time alone to process a stunning realization: that the Sicily that was described to me, the Sicily I had learned about from others is nonexistent. At my more private times on my first trip, I am repeatedly comparing what I see and hear to all that I was told about Palermo, Sicily, Sicilians, and the world my grandparents left. It did not take long for me to determine that the Sicily I carried in me from the meager stories told by grandparents, great aunts, and uncles, cousins, and friends was pure fiction. No such Sicily exists and likely never did. The Sicily I am discovering is more than, and other than, I ever could have expected.

First and foremost, I'd heard stories about extreme poverty. But the Sicily of today is apparently without destitution. Yes, poverty does exist in Sicily, both in the towns and on the countryside. But everyone I see is fed and decently clothed. There are panhandlers, gypsy children, and street people, more part of a class of performance artists than of the truly destitute. No one is starving in Sicily. No one is, in the truest sense, a beggar. (This was not always so.)

I encounter gypsy women on two separate occasions

working similar gigs. Both are heavily shrouded in black, clutching rosary beads, and nearly prostrate on the thresholds of churches. As I come near enough to enter La Martarona, a Palermo church sentried by one of the gypsy women, the woman squeals and weeps in a high, operatic fashion, bewailing the thoroughly miserable lot that the fates have handed her.

Somehow, both women recognize me as a tourist because neither of them bothers to perform their swoons for native Sicilian church visitors or passersby. Perhaps they realize that Sicilians, the masters of such histrionics, will regard their verismo opera as the performance of rank amateurs.

I learn that Sicilians unlike the gypsy women, will not likely bemoan poverty without some humor in the retelling. Hardship was/is the fortune of many in Sicily. So, Sicilians will not bore their friends and neighbors with the overt suffering they share. Emoting to their peers required humor. In fact, Sicilians do a great deal of smiling and laughing. They are show-offs and terrific storytellers. They have not relinquished an oral tradition. And laughter has aided their survival.

Heartbreak, on the other hand, is quite another matter. In the world there are all sorts of heartbreak. In Sicily, there is only one. Heartbreak is the loss of your beloved.

If a Sicilian loses a child, he or she suffers in silence. (Well, little is truly silent in Sicily.) Stoicism in grief is more in keeping with the Sicilian character but not without its requisite theatricality. The parents and family members of the dead child will be silent while the rest of the community is rife with discussion of how that mother is or is not coping; how hurt is so evident in the face of the dead child's once cheerful father.

If Sicilians are to weep and wail it is over lost love.

Above: The Cathedral of St. Rosalie in Palermo

Left: The Church of St. Domenico at Entry to the Market of Vucciria in Palermo

Woman in the Kalso in Palermo

THREE

*Irritability, bad moods, and outbursts of affect are the
classic symptoms of chronic virtuousness.*

—Carl Jung, Answer to Job

My other Sicilian family is the family of my first love,
Dominick. At this writing, Dominick has been dead
more than twenty years. We met as undergraduates. He grew
up in Westchester County above New York City. He was quiet
and studious. I was a wild-man poet.

Having a boyfriend or lover was the furthest thing from
my mind. I had no notion that anyone would put up with me,
and I hadn't the patience to put up with anyone else. Yet, (and
there is always a "yet" at such turning points) something held
us together, bumpy as our life together was.

Falling in love is a very deceptive bit of business by which
one thinks one is in charge until one is no longer. "This is
okay," I said to myself one morning. I said it once again on
another morning because things seemed to be even better
than okay. Then on another morning weeks later, I awaken
next to this warm snoozing presence and realize that
separation at this stage is unthinkable.

Sicily has volcanoes, and surviving their eruptions may
be some sort of training for falling in love. The unexpected
explosions, the tectonic shifts, the irreversible changes of the

landscape…maybe Sicilians are addicted to such romantic and geological upheavals because of the frequent occurrences of volcanic upheavals on their island.

The whole sex and romance thing is central to being Sicilian. I do not trust a person who cannot be a complete fool for love. My parents had a volcanic romance. They were not very good friends after more than sixty years together, but they remained madly in love until the days they died.

Dominick's family was very close. They spent much of their time together. In fact, their lives were lived in order to spend time together. They had their foibles, but mostly they enjoyed one another's company.

My own family's mission was to create as much distance as possible between one another. We all needed air from the closeness of physical proximity from our tiny apartment. We needed to escape the tyranny of my father's self-centeredness and my mother's need to continually foster his outbursts.

Adulthood improved things with my own family but only a little.

With Dominick's people, I learned so much because time and space allowed. Learning takes some amount of openness, leisure, and calm.

On my first visit to Sicily, I discovered that Dominick's first and last names are all over Palermo. His face was on a hundred Palermitans I passed on the street.

Ironically, Dominick preferred France to Italy. He thought the food and culture were better.

Dominick and his family endured every bit as much internalized Siciliano-phobia as my Kansas City family. But though all of our years together, they were more family to me than my own.

Once while watching 60 Minutes with Dominik's parents a leading gangster from my hometown appeared on the screen.

I identified him by name before the reporter had. Dominick's mother was shocked. "How do you know who he is?"

I told her that I knew more than who he was; I knew him. The Italian community in Kansas City was relatively small. We all knew one another. This made her very uneasy. I did not go on to tell her how many of the young men with whom I grew up had done time.

Nor did I tell her that a guy I actually hung out with in my teens was we believed in the witness protection program. After watching Tony Soprano say that the man his sister had killed in an earlier episode was in the witness protection program, it dawned on me that this pal from my teenage years might, in fact, be dead. In any case, he had disappeared.

Dominick and I frequently went to Arthur Avenue in the Bronx to shop for groceries. Arthur Avenue is one of the diaspora neighborhoods in the United States that look enough like Sicily or Southern Italy that you might believe you've crossed the Atlantic rather than the Cross Bronx Expressway. Except for the size of the cars (always double and triple parked down the street), you'd think you were at the Agora or marketplace of Siracusa where the town meets the tiny island of Ortygia.

Fun Fact. Regardless which side of the Atlantic they are on, Sicilians will park an automobile anywhere. In the States, it is actually more ridiculous because they're not trying to tuck away some tiny Fiat. We're generally talking the likes of a Lincoln Town Car or a Sedan DeVille on Arthur Avenue.

If we arrived at the market early enough in the day, produce brokers in the middle of the street were doing business with grocers and restaurateurs. One rotund and bellowing gentleman trussed into an undersized, copiously stained work apron his swollen fingers grasping a clutch of twenties, fifties and hundreds worked four deals at once. "No, you do not get his price because you do not buy as much as he does." He grabs a breath. "You do business like him and I will give you his price."

Dominick's mother says to me, "He shouldn't have all that money out on the street like this."

"Oh, Sue," I retort, "I don't think anyone's going to take anything from that guy."

On Arthur Avenue, we bought bread, produce, and canned tomatoes. A cheese vendor named Mike had all of his husky lookalike sons behind the counter hawking cheese with him. When someone asked if this boy or that was his son, he'd say yes and grab the butch twenty-something fellow and kiss him smack on the lips. It always got a laugh.

It occurs to me (as I ride the train from Agrigento to Palermo), that I learned many things from Dominick and his family in our nearly twenty years together. If I have grown up, if I have become a man of strength and compassion (and as I write this riding a Sicilian train from Agrigento to Palermo), if I have become a man of honor, Dominick and his family had much to do with that.

FOUR
(A Memory...maybe!)

In the summer of 1994, my father underwent heart surgery. By the time I arrived at the hospital in Kansas City, many of my family members were already gathered outside the surgical suite.

There were maybe six or seven of us surrounding my mother in the corner of the waiting room. Our familial encampment was mingled with smaller groups of twos and threes of sober Midwesterners who chatted quietly and demurely as if they were in church. By the looks on their faces, I could see they thought we were a batch of maniacs.

The waspy midwesterners were right and righteous in their soft-spoken concern for the well-being of their loved ones in surgery. We, on the other hand, were Spanos. It was not as if we failed to appreciate the gravity of the situation that day in the surgical waiting room. We certainly outnumbered the Midwesterners. It is just that the Spanos are Sicilians, and we are loud. We are loud even when we are seriously concerned—maybe more so.

My sister thought we might be offending some of these people and suggested we quiet down. What a dreamer! We weren't going to shut up. The only way to quiet us down was to thin out our crowd.

My cousin Mary and her husband Joe were there.
Mary and Joe were retired from the produce business. As
mentioned, produce is what most of my father's side did when
they arrived in the United States. Mary was my mother's best
friend. She was also my father's first cousin. She introduced
my parents. I guess I owe my very existence to her.

"Did they feed you on the plane, honey?" Cousin Mary
asked me in her husky voice which sounds more like a
prizefighter than the sweet woman I know her to be.

"No, just coffee," I replied.

My father would not be out of surgery for at least another
three hours. Mary and Joe were heading over to see another
of our cousins, Bea, my oldest living relative and a first cousin
to Mary and my father. Why didn't I go along with them and
get some lunch and say hello to cousin Bea whom I had not
seen since I was a boy?

A woman who had outlived two of her five children,
Bea was ninety-five years old and used a walker but was as
articulate and as mentally sharp as a much younger woman.
All of her children had matriculated from the produce
business to the grocery business with some amount of success.

While with Cousin Bea, I questioned her about our shared
relatives and their arrivals in the United States. Bea's mother
and my grandmother and Cousin Mary's father—the Inzerillos—
were all siblings. The Inzerillos and the Spanos, Cousin Bea told
me were from La Vucciria, the market in Palermo.

This was the first time I had heard that story. No one talked
about Sicily. When I was very young and would say I wanted to
go to Sicily one day, I was told it was old and dirty, and I probably
wouldn't like it. Not until my adulthood did I understand
that they discouraged an interest in Sicily because they had
been painfully poor in Sicily and without a single opportunity.
Nothing seemed likely to change so they left the country.

That day, I told Cousin Bea that I wanted to go to Sicily. She said I was not to miss Monreale. That was where her late husband was from. The cathedral was beautiful. I must go there.

I had already planned to go there. But it was the market La Vucciria that kept popping up again and again in what I have come to believe was a meaningful coincidence.

Before I made it to Sicily, for example, I visited Asheboro, North Carolina where I had lunch in a cubby-hole of a pizza joint. The owner was from Palermo. I told him my family were Palermitans and that they had come from the market La Vucciria. He taught me how to say the word correctly softening the "v" to almost a "u" sound.

Then I happened upon a book in Italian that talked about all the markets of Palermo and introduced me to the famous painting by Renato Guttuso entitled La Vucciria. I loved that particular painting at first sight. And after investigating Guttuso further, I discovered works that filled the senses to overflowing.

It was not simply his palette of colors, his style of composition or his extraordinary subject matter, I felt Guttuso was my kin.
He seemed to me an artist who demanded the full truth in his life and work.

I visited Sicily for the first time in 2010. By then, the generation before me had all gone. I was left with memories of conversations to go on. I was staying at a bed and breakfast on Ruggero Settimo right off Politeama in the center of Palermo. My innkeeper Giuseppe was interested in why I was there. I told him I wanted to see the markets. "Before you see Capella Palatina?" he asked.

"Yes," I replied, "I want to see La Vucciria."

"Oh, that's an old market. Do not go there."

I explained that I was not going to shop. This was the

place where my father's family came from.

"Then, you must go there," he now insisted.

In late afternoon, from Via Maqueda, I cut across the un-trafficked promenade at Ruggero Settimo to Via Roma and in a few blocks, I arrive at the Church of San Domenico— La Vucciria's front door.

The word "vucciria" is an evolved mispronunciation of the French word boucherie, meaning butchery. The market is the very heart of the city. It has been there for over seven hundred years.

It is not simply a food market. It is an everything market. Closer to an Arab souk or bazaar than a western style farmer's market.

As I descend by way of La Vucciria's narrow curving streets, a damp black grimy mixture of garbage and God-knows-what abrades the soles of my shoes. The smells change with every step, over-ripe fruit, frying fish, stale beer, cheap cologne, cigar smoke, sausage cooking in the tiny interior piazza. The colors shift from bright to darkly muted as the sun moves overhead light and shadow dodging in and out of the buildings.

Every vertical surface available thick with peeling handbills and placards layered upon each other, a modern fresco plastered over the ancient. The graffiti defies any I've seen even in New York for its shear ribaldry and inspired rage. And, just a little above arm's reach is an occasional shrine to the Virgin, Santa Rosalia, San Domenico or the Sacred Heart. Some are tidy and adorned with votive lights and plastic flowers. Others are dirty and neglected.

Young people spill out the front door of a bar into a street meant for donkeys rather than cars, trucks, Vespas, and bicyclists trying to get where they're going at quitting time. The swarm from the bar are drinking, laughing, and smoking. It seems nearly everyone in this glamorous crowd is smoking. Most are fashionably dressed in stark contrast to the dilapidation of their surroundings. And, rest assured, everyone in this crowd is coming on to at least one other person in the crowd.

It all seems so familiar. I've never set foot here in my life but seem to know my way around. Nothing feels foreign.

I tell my logical self all the likely explanations for this instant familiarity. This is where my family came from. These people look like me and my family members. At some primal level, they may give off an endemic or aboriginal scent of my people, my tribe. Then there is the most glaring fact: the names.

Many Sicilians and Palermitans emigrated to my hometown. Many of the names on signs and businesses in La Vucciria were the same as those I saw walking through The City Market in Kansas City or down Fifth Street in the North End. I am also struck by so many parallel manifestations of daily living.

But the most striking is at an intersection on Via Roma just outside the market. A store with Spanò on the sign appears on one corner. (In Sicily, my name has an accento grave on the "ò" which was likely lost in New Orleans, my grandfather's port of entry into the United States.) Across the side street a business with my grandmother's maiden name Inzerillo.

Since that first visit, whenever I return to Sicily I go back to wander through La Vucciria. The question I asked myself that first day, the question I continue to ask is, how can I remember a place I have never visited before in my life?

Swiss psychotherapist Carl Jung used the term "collective unconscious" to describe his idea of inherited traits, intuitions, and primordial wisdom. More recently, scientists have found "compelling evidence" for the biological transmission of memory. Did my DNA bestow upon me knowledge of my ancestors lives that I carry within me? Perhaps when I was born the knowledge of La Vucciria came "factory installed."

From wherever my knowledge, comfort with, and immediate passion for this place came I will likely never know in this lifetime. One thing is certain: Not only is La Vucciria the beating heart of Palermo; it is also mine.

La Vucciria by Renato Guttuso

FIVE

...excommunication is a necessary and useful consequence.
—Carl Jung, Psychology and Alchemy

For my partner Carlus and me, Giuseppe's house is an island of quiet amid the noise and traffic of Palermo. Carlus loves our room with its grand bed, a bejeweled chandelier, and terrazzo floors. The whole flat is decorated with very elegant paintings. Not too Baroque or overdone but with great refinement. Giuseppe is himself a man of true refinement.

He's an old-style remnant of aristocratic Palermitan in a world that has become over time much less affluent but no less urbane. The Palazzo came to him through his mother's family. I will get him to tell me more of his family.

At breakfast, I talk with a young Frenchman. He is Hervé. He and his girlfriend are from Aix-en-Provence. He works in technology. We talk marketing, Apple, Microsoft, Google, Skype, the Esperanto of the young. Hervé and his girlfriend are in transit to Stromboli to camp out on the hillside of the active volcano on this island.

As Carlus and I wander the grounds of the Norman Palace, the place is besieged with bands of students and I can't help but notice that Sicilian young people are beautiful. The girls are pretty, but the young men are exquisite. They all know this, of course. Regardless of their economic station, they are all royalty for the few years of their coming-of-age. This is a generally acknowledged fact of life in Sicily. Families indulge the beauty and marriagability of their adolescents. This is the order of things in Sicily.

Probably why I love Sicily the most as elegant as it is, as much culture as much history—nowhere else on earth is there as much history—there is still an aspect that will never be tamed. It is going to be wild. It is going to be out of control. It is going to be a bumpy ride, but that's what makes it so beautiful.

—Michela Musolino, Sicilian-American Folksinger

Sicilians seem to look wonderful all the time. Beauty is a very important part of Sicilian life. Beauty holds promise. It holds promise of a better day, it holds promise of prosperity, it holds promise of love. Is this show business? You bet it is. Show business is a great part of the Sicilian persona, this public self that has such dignity and so much charm.

A beauty born of harshness affects everything in Sicily. No matter how dark the Sicilian soul may be, it is the sun— so present a part of a Sicilian's daily life—that bathes the darkness, washing it away for those moments of dazzling brilliance.

Sicily is made of stone. Every walking surface is hard. You can't walk anywhere outside in Sicily without finding a hardness or an unevenness underfoot. So many stones protrude from streets and sidewalks. As I walk, they make my feet hurt. In the evening and for a while in the morning, they make my back ache. If walking in four-inch heels becomes an Olympic sport, Sicily will provide all the gold medalists.

The Norman Kingdom of Sicily was one of the few bright spots in the history of the island. If the mosaics from the Norman Kingdom are full of indescribable beauty, they are also unimaginable artistic achievements. So many tiny pieces of ceramic placed individually to create an image, a highlight, an entire narrative.

For the Capella Palatina, the royal chapel adjacent to the Palazzo Normani in Palermo, King Roger II (1130-54) used Persian and Arab artisans to create an environment capable of conveying a peak experience in a relatively small place. "Think of this place," Carlus says as we are leaving the totally mosaicked Chapel, "full of lighted candles, monks chanting, incense wafting through. Anybody now or in Medieval times would be thoroughly compelled to believe. Experiencing this place would close the deal for God."

Not far from Capella Palatina, Carlus and I enter the church of San Giovanni degli Ermiti. (The church, with its typically Islamic domes, was a mosque originally.) This simple, austere monastic enclosure made of roughhewn stone seems to be a cluster of man-made caves in the very center of the city. The rooms are dank and severe in their dark hardness. The space for common prayer is anything but inspiring. I can only imagine the misery of kneeling for midnight prayers on such a cold hard surface for any length of time.

Within the cloister is a garden sequestered totally from the outside except for the sky. The garden's shade is dappled with sunlight. Sitting on garden benches Carlus and I were cool, quiet and relaxed. The rows are planted with traditional herbs as one might have found in a monk's garden from the early middle ages. San Giovanni degli Ermiti was a gift from a contemplative past surviving into the present, an oasis from the usual downtown mayhem of Palermo.

Later as we enter the church at Monreale, a wedding is underway. The nave is an immense corridor of mosaic. The fifty or so people who make up the wedding party seem a few blocks away within the huge sanctuary of Christ the Pantokrator.

If Capella Palatina's beauty is somehow tied to the intimacy of the place, the church attached to a Benedictine monastery at Monreale possesses a grandness that is very much tied to the vastness of the space. Built by William II (or William the Good), Monreale is visually over the top. Critics have termed it "crass." Probably because I am of Sicilian origin, I find it staggering. Or maybe I just have a higher threshold for extravagance than others.

The entire structure seems much more Middle Eastern and Arabic than it does Western or Italian. Biblical narratives line the upper walls of the interior. I love the naïve quality of the mosaics. Carlus especially liked the images depicting the resurrection of Lazarus. Jesus seems to be sending a life beam from his eyes that is reanimating Martha's and Mary's rotting brother. To me, the mosaics bear a hint of primitiveness that suggests a comic strip. Nonetheless, the images feel very authentic, emanating from a profound connection to the spiritual.

Not twenty minutes into our visit the organ begins to pipe the Bridal Chorus from Lohengrin, the playing of which I was told all my life was forbidden in Roman Catholic Churches. A very Sicilian lesson is embedded in this event—in the combined sentiments regarding the sweetness of the wedding itself and Sicilians playing fast and loose with church rules, or, for that matter, any rules to have exactly what they want.

Travelers visit religious sites. It's part of what we do. Temples, mosques, shrines, churches, holy places of every stripe. At an earlier time in my life, I might have remembered churches better than markets. Lacking any religious faith whatsoever would have been no excuse. I was once dazzled by architectural achievement in the service of faith. I no longer view the thousands of churches I have visited over my travels with such secular reverence. A church must have something to say to me right now in this very present.

In a Palermo eatery on Via Vittorio Emmanuele, Carlus and I are enjoying lunch when a very effeminate local boy of maybe sixteen or seventeen enters. The young man buys a cold drink and sits at a table to drink it and reads a book he's carrying. In less than ten minutes the young man departs. Several of the Sicilians in the place both men and women roll their eyes and giggle. Apparently, to the remaining patrons in the place, Carlus and I are not gay because we are not observed as such. These seemingly friendly people are not aware of the cruelty of this posture. At least they didn't make fun of the young man in his presence.

I don't like what I've witnessed, but it was still better than what transpired in Kansas City when I was growing up. Before I fully understood that I was gay, I saw neighborhood boys bullying others who they guessed might be gay. We can create all sorts of explanations for this behavior, but ultimately it is abusive whether or not the object of ridicule is in the room. And like so much else in Sicily it has its very own smell.

During our walks, Carlus and I notice at least four people with disabilities who are accompanied by very attentive parents or siblings. I think about this for a moment. In America we are always in our cars. We do not get close enough to others to see into their lives.

One afternoon I am ambling alone near Politeama.

An old couple, likely in their eighties, are walking with a developmentally disabled son. The son is possibly in his fifties. The three walk with locked arms, the son in the middle. I hear his mother call him "Fausto." I can see that his breathing is severely labored and he has almost no muscle tone.

Right in front of the MacDonald's at Piazza St. Oliva, Fausto's legs simply collapse under him and his parents struggle to prevent him from sprawling onto the heavily trafficked sidewalk. But they are simply incapable of holding him up. I rush over to ask if I can help. They welcome the offer.

Fausto's legs simply refuse to obey. He keeps crumbling like a dishrag. And Fausto is a big man. He is heavy for me, not to mention his geriatric parents. After prolonged pushing and pulling, we finally get Fausto completely upright and moving forward. I introduce myself to his parents, who tell me they had good friends named Spanò.

Before I go, I tell Fausto how well he is doing. I repeat, "Sta bene." Fausto replies "Bella!" because he's staring at a fashionable, round-hipped young woman posing in the customary Sicilian four-inch platform shoes. She has no idea that Fausto, his parents, and I are on the same planet as she.

Some aspects of Sicilian life are predictably consistent.

Christiane's arrival changes the dynamics so much. Carlus and I travel together as anonymous watchers. With Christiane's arrival, we are a trio of revelers.

Giuseppe loves Christiane. She is a beautiful French woman; he is a Sicilian man. Based on even her slightest of eye movements, Giuseppe is at her side asking how he may help. He is very attentive to Carlus and me, but not at all like he is to Christiane.

It is late afternoon. Christiane is going to rest and afterward, we will go out to dinner to a place Giuseppe has recommended. Carlus must eat gluten-free foods, so Giuseppe has chosen a restaurant that purports to serve gluten-free entrees. I can hear him engaged in a telephonic arm-wrestling match with the person on the other end of the line as he makes our reservation, insisting that the they will have gluten-free pasta for Carlus. The reservation is made.

The three of us arrive at the restaurant early and find the door locked. The lights are on and we can see through the heavy, beveled glass door that the dining room is completely empty. It is somewhat early for a Sicilian dinner, so we go look for a drink. After nearly an hour, we are back at the same beautiful and completely locked restaurant door. An old couple pulls up in a car. The woman jumps out, tries the door and asks us when the place will open. We look at her in a befuddled and touristic manner. She turns in a huff at our stupidity and jumps back into the car. They drive away.

As we stand there not knowing what to do, a passerby points to a doorbell very low on the right. Christiane pushes the doorbell. We hear a loud chime and in seconds someone comes running up from a stairway in the dining room and lets us in. He only says Giuseppe's last name in a questioning tone. We say yes. He then says as clearly as a Shakespearean actor, "Gluten-free?" Again, we say yes.

We are taken downstairs to a full dining room and seated at a table. As busboys bring water, bread, silver, and so forth, each says as he performs his specific duty, "Gluten-free?" We say yes, each time. I point to Carlus who is fair-skinned and redheaded.

Now each service person approaching the table not only asks, "Gluten-free?" but they also turn to Carlus and ask, "Tedesco?" (Italian for German). The wine steward tries to engage him by speaking German language. Carlus continues to insist he is "Americano" without much acceptance of this reality on the parts of the help.

Another member of the staff comes to the table announcing enthusiastically, "Becker! Becker!". Most of the dining room is now looking toward our table and repeating at various levels of audibility "Becker! Becker! Boris Becker. Boris Becker!" Carlus may slightly favor the German tennis champ, but not nearly to the point as to disrupt an entire restaurant. Nonetheless, everyone is completely agreeable, and the meal moves forward pleasurably.

A large family at the next table is celebrating something. There are at least twenty of them of every age, from babies to great-grandparents. Everyone is dressed for the occasion. They are finishing up and very likely have been in the restaurant since early afternoon. It's now around nine p.m. A cake is brought to their table and presented to a boy of about eight years old. The cake is huge and quite ornately decorated. It looks like a Sicilian Baroque church.

A waiter then lifts the cake away from the boy and waltzes it around the huge table of family members. Everyone oohs and aahs. Then he starts showing the cake around the entire dining room. When he gets to us, he explains that it is the boy's First Holy Communion.

At some point, we finally disabuse the restaurant staff of the notion that Carlus is German or, for that matter, Boris Becker. And he did get his gluten-free pasta. At the end of our meal, right after coffee is set at our table, one of waitstaff places small digestif glasses in front of each of us. Then, the head waiter places a huge bottle of grappa in front of Carlus and announces, "Gluten-free!" First the restaurant staff then the entire dining room bursts into loud laughter.

We rise from our table around midnight. As we leave,

everyone is saying their goodbyes to us. Most of the Holy Communion party-goers are still at their table. The small children are curled on couches along an opposite wall, snoozing like angels.

We find ourselves on a Palermo street named for Richard Wagner. I begin singing "Lohengrin." Carlus is not a fan of my spontaneous public operatic performances that are generally brought on by grappa or the like. After his more than vociferous objection, I turn to him and say, "Gluten-free, Herr Becker!"

In the morning as the three of us are departing Palermo, Carlus is stricken with sinus issues likely related to Palermo pollution. We are on a bus to Trapani. Carlus sleeps the whole trip. On arriving in Trapani, I find a town that is more a resort than a fishing village. Worse yet, it is a cruise ship stop.

We check into a bed and breakfast with ancient stone staircases as steep as a house painter's ladder. Our innkeeper has Diana Krall playing through the common area. Carlus is sick and fussy like a three-year-old. Diana is familiar to him. As she sings that she "knows a little bit about a lot of things..." we haul our bags up what we believe to be the final, ominously steep flight of stairs to our room. In our room, we find another flight of steps, equally steep, to our bathroom. I can imagine my ascent and descent of this scala santa for a 3 a.m. piss.

Carlus continues to suffer from his sinus issues. We get him antibiotics. Christiane and I head off to the water. The day is a warm mix of clouds and sun. And it's quiet here. This is rest I very much need.

Even without any articulated discussion of the past, when Christiane and I are alone together, we remember.

As I've mentioned, Christiane is French-born. She and her

husband Jim, a lanky engineer from Texas, and their two-year-old daughter Melanie lived outside our back door when Dominick and I moved to the Virginia suburbs. Melanie introduced herself to us and conned us out of ice cream and Chinese food for Saturday lunch for years to come.

On an autumn afternoon, Jim hollered across a collapsing fence that we eventually rebuilt together. I heard "I have a son!" float across our shared property line with a pride reserved for fathers of sons.

By the time his son Steven was two, Jim was in his late thirties and was diagnosed with a swift and ravaging cancer. In six months, he left us. Less than four years later, Dominick was gone.

Christiane and I were often up late listening to the harsh rattle of Edith Piaf. "Non, je ne regrette rien," the little sparrow wept on our behalves. We tried to explain it to ourselves on many nights over many years. We never truly succeeded. I moved to North Carolina and met Carlus. She eventually remarried.

Since we were in our thirties then, Christiane and I healed our hearts by sunning ourselves on many a beach. We are in our sixties now and our bond is strong. We buried husbands together. We are members of a secret society. We are the ones no longer capable of crying over spilt milk.

We visit the mountaintop town of Erice. The weather is bright and clear but the wind is downright cold. Erice is fascinating yet still very touristy. I am happy, though, to be in a more out-of-the-way place.

The next day we take the ferry to Favignana where I am mesmerized. Fishermen sit in tiny blue boats at the port where we dock.

Favignana is one of the Egadi island chain off the coast of Trapani. It is more rocky and rugged than even the Sicilian mainland. The structures are from every era as far back as the Phoenicians. There are cows and sheep, piles of rocks and old quarries, and so much white stone called "tufo." Tufo is a soft stone that has been mined extensively on the island, leaving giant pits below the sea winds that have been turned into lemon groves. It is no wonder that the Sicilian flag is on a half-yellow field. The yellow of the lemons, the sunflowers, the sun itself—so much of Sicily is yellow.

The blue-green clarity of the water sloshes its pulsing cuff onto a craggy and jagged basalt coastline. Seabirds in sizes, shapes, and varieties as I have never seen before soar and plummet against a sky that rivals only the sea for its exquisiteness. Abruptly the smell of salt water becomes all that there is.

On our return, we are midway between Trapani and Favignana. I glimpse Trapani, a remote station on an island. Yet compared to Favignana, a more remote island station, Trapani is a bustling metropolis.

Sicily is becoming a metaphor for my less and less unconscious rejection of modernity—a simultaneous acceptance and rejection of the world as I find it.

I do not want to return to the States. I dream of flying home and beginning the process of repatriating myself to Sicily. As I write today however, that fantasy fades in the realities of my bonds to home, family, and the United States.

With so many flowering trees and vehicular exhaust, Palermo is a very tough place to be if you suffer from allergies. Carlus has been suffering through varying states of ill-health. My eyes are bloodshot, not all of which can be blamed on drinking.

I self-medicate my allergies with Sicilian coffee. In the States, I can drink maybe three cups of coffee in a day. But three cups of Giuseppe's coffee may require a medical intervention for the shakes. I know now why Etna erupts: They pour Sicilian coffee into the crater.

Let's agree at the outset that I am not easily rendered speechless. This afternoon I'm sipping a cold drink in a cafe in Palermo when I'm approached by an elderly German couple. Both are short and round and rather red-faced, maybe in their early eighties.

The man, who seems very affable, approaches me speaking with almost comedic, Colonel Klink-accented English, "You are American?" His wife stands by him grinning ear-to-ear.

"Yes."

"What is the meaning of this word…metrosexual?"

I sit a while staring into the space of the sun-filled afternoon. I haven't a clue what to say to him. Then I wonder why he thinks I might know the meaning versus hundreds of Sicilian practitioners of said term, all easily a third my age with a good facility of either English or German. Finally, I tell him I don't know, but when I find out I'll get back to him.

At that moment, I decide to make a film about Sicily.

SIX

When I'm raising money to make a film, a great many of the people I know treat me as if I'm having some sort of personal tragedy—like I've been arrested for exposing myself in public or I've attempted suicide. They seem superficially sympathetic, but they do their best to steer clear of me. For a personal tragedy or for trying to fund a film, I'm always surprised by who steps up.

At the time of this particular chunk of writing, my Sicily documentary was not funded. I was nuts with distraction. I'd nearly lost my ability to focus on anything but the money for the film. I didn't feel like bathing or shaving until the project was secure. I wished I could stop eating until my film was funded. I would be skinny again!

On my second trip to Sicily, I learn that with a hand-held camera, you can shoot just about anywhere in Sicily. You are regarded as a tourist. As soon as you set up a tripod, you magically transform into a production company in the eyes of the authorities and require a production permit from the regional Film and Tourism office.

I'm joined in Sicily by my friend Floyd who is now living in Spain. He has always been willing to help me with any of my wild schemes. As he is unpacking, he removes from his bag a meticulously crocheted white table runner. He made it as a gift for my partner Carlus. He crocheted it during long stretches in the hospital in Spain. Floyd is battling cancer.

The next morning, Floyd awakens early. He is in the atrium where breakfast is served. He has finished his breakfast and is instructing a half-dozen elderly women from Puglia on the varieties of ways to fold napkins for the table and how to artfully fold the end of the toilet paper roll. After Floyd's lesson, the ladies from Puglia applaud.

After breakfast, we go thread-and-yarn shopping in the Ballaro Market. He asks me to choose the yarn that he will make into a scarf for me.

We have lunch in the market. The woman who brings lunch shares my last name. With no more research than this, Floyd declares the woman and me to be cousins. My newfound Spanò cousin sends us off with a huge bag of fresh cherries.

After a circuitous bus ride into the hills, we are at the Duomo at Monreale. We are shooting some preliminary video for a fundraising screener for the documentary. I rarely shoot my own material because I do not have a steady hand. So I open my tripod. As soon as the tripod's three rubber-covered feet hit the cathedral floor, we're busted.

Surrounded by cathedral guards, Floyd calmly explains that I had Parkinson's Disease (I don't) and lack a steady hand. That's why I need the tripod. The officials are buying none of Floyd's compassionate plea. We are summarily ejected from the Duomo of Monreale.

Outside the church, Floyd ponders aloud, "These guys deal with Sicilians every day. They had probably heard that one before."

When we check the footage later we smile. Despite the guards' intrusion, we have enough for a promotional video for the documentary.

In Sicily, Catholicism has a profound influence on the senses often at the expense of reason. I believe the Church has so shaped the Sicilian imagination that the simple truth can be horrifyingly painful. This is clearly part of the Sicilian character that I inherited.

Camille Paglia has written, "Italy restores the pagan theatricality of western identity," and nowhere is this more the case than in Sicily. Sicilians express their religion in very concrete and sensual ways.

I can never quite make up my mind if Sicilians are very, very religious or if they're just pretending.

—Veronica Hughes Di Grigoli, Author and Sicily Blogger

Religion is truly a conundrum in Sicily. I confess that I love the barefaced idolatry or sympathetic magic of Sicilian Catholicism. It is a magic that assumes a person or thing can be supernaturally affected by proclaiming the name of something or venerating an object representing it. It is so much like the magical realism of Latin American writers. I believe the impulses for both sympathetic magic and magical realism come from the same source—this need to demonstrate faith, hope, and love in a very public way.

They externalize a faith that is almost shouted in a special way. Seeing it on camera, it truly shows in the faces of the people.

—Mario Nicotra, Sicilian Theologian

Many of these practices come from classical mythology or pagan cults inserted into Roman Catholicism. Maybe Christianity inserted itself upon preexisting pagan rites. This is not a claim I am necessarily qualified to make, but I believe the connections exist and flourish to this day.

Whenever battles were fought to eradicate paganism from Christian practices in Sicily, Christianity lost decisively. Edicts to destroy temples across the island were simply ignored. Some structures, like those in Siracusa, were consecrated as Catholic churches, but a great many remained standing and continued to be places of veneration to their original pagan deities.

You know we are a goddess island.

—Gioia Timpanelli, Sicilian-American Author and Storyteller

Persephone is Sicily's Greek patron goddess (Prosperina in her Roman identity). Persephone embodies Sicily's abundance, fertility, and the volatility of this volcanic island. This goddess was an easy segue to the Blessed Virgin.

It is the devotion to Mary; it is the worship of a woman, the mother of God, that lies at the heart of Catholic expression for southern Italians and certainly here in Sicily, and it is this mix of religious devotion and sexual desire that lies at the heart of southern Italian culture.

—Thomas Puleo, Author and Scholar

Each Sicilian town has its patron saint. Most of these saints are female. Saint Agatha is Catania's patron. She is revered with an ardor and gusto that I have only seen displayed elsewhere in Sicily by soccer fans. Her saint's day is a party that could rival Carnevale in Rio.

The saint that protects Catania is Agatha. Agatha is not a man. If you go in the Dome of Catania there's a little Jesus Christ..., in a corner. Then it is Agatha everywhere, everywhere.

—Carlo Condarelli, Sicilian Folk Musician and Catania Native

We can read in the Lives of the Saints that St. Agatha suffered wicked martyrdom. Her breasts were cut off. This foul, sadistic deed was then depicted in religious art. In Catania itself, there are many grisly renderings of Agatha's untimely end.

It seems to me that there is very little here from Christianity because it slips immediately into fanaticism." Catanians live adjacent to Mount Etna the most active volcano in Europe. They see Agatha as a protector. There are peoplewho say that the lava was stopped when Saint Agatha extended her veil.

—Mario Nicotra, Sicilian Theologian

Agatha in Italian is Agathina, means little Agatha, "In Sicilian this is Aiethina, so Aiethina, and the ancient name of Etna is Aietna, so is Aiethina and Aietna. So maybe she's linked with the mountain. Maybe people they are devoted to the power of this mountain...This is a miracle. This is a chemistry, it is alchemy. And it is up there.

—Carlo Condarelli, Sicilian Folk Musician and Catania Native

Saint Agatha in religious history suffered a terrible fate. Her breasts were cut off. Because this happened to a saint, this sadistic act could then be portrayed in religious art. We could do some beautiful breast-like cakes, sometimes even topped with a little cherry. This was a kind of sanctified, beatified pornography which was permitted even inside the convent.

—Joseph Farrell, Author and Sicilian Scholar

More pagan than Christian, the Day of the Dead is still a pretty significant holiday in Sicily. It is celebrated a bit like Christmas and happens on November 2nd, what we call All Souls Day, two days after Halloween. The Day of the Dead is not an unhappy occasion. Families come out to decorate loved ones' graves with flowers, to visit, and in some cases to even picnic at the cemetery. It is a cause for celebration, an occasion to be reunited with your ancestors.

Dias metros, is very important in the Spanish world. The dead bring presents to the children. There are special cookies in the form of bones. Once there was a tradition of a kind of picnicking at the cemetery. It was a kind of family gathering. There was this continuity between death and life, and here is all about death and life. The dead are not dead. There is still continuity.

—Nicoletta Polo, Palermitana and Guardian
   of Lampedusa Legacy

SEVEN

Going to Sicily is better than going to the moon.
—Gabriel Garcìa Màrquez

The moon lives in the lining of your skin.
—Pablo Neruda

The Catanian composer Vincenzo Bellini wrote a now-famous hymn to the Lady in the Moon in Act I of his opera Norma. Norma sings "Casta Diva" (chaste goddess) to the white and distant deity that makes us all crazy.

The day before I returned to the States, my friend Sabrina emailed me to say she had arranged a meeting for me with a Mr. Enzo of the Sicilian Office of Tourism and Cinema. She included an address, a time, and a place.

It's twenty minutes prior to the purported appointment, and I'm walking on Via Notabartolo, an old Palermo boulevard flanked by condo buildings, office buildings, and venerable palazzi, some of which are still residences and others that have been turned into God knows what.

I am searching for #11 Via Notabartolo. I find #9, #13, #15, but no #11. In Sicily #13 is not bad luck It is, in fact, good luck, and it's there in all its glory but no #11.

A building that looked as if it might be a residence flew the Italian, Sicilian and European Union flags. I'm guessing that those flags over one of the various doors at #9 might be my pick. I see a woman walking through the door and follow her. Inside people are coming and going. It is, after all, a Monday morning.

At a counter that appears to be a security desk sit three Sicilian men, each representing stages of human life. A freckled-faced young man dressed in designer jeans, a sheer white dress shirt, a blue tie and khaki jacket might have been as old as twenty-five. The other two are not so nattily dressed but also in jacket and tie. We'll call one "Forty-or-so" and the other "Sixty-ish." I approach Signor Sixty-ish and, in my faulty Italian, begin to ask him the whereabouts of Signor Enzo. He gives me an expression I rarely get in Italy but have received many times in France. It's a look that says, "Please do not speak my language because I am not even going to try to understand you."

So I stop and launch into my explanation in English. Immediately, all three men focus on me as if I'm Abe Lincoln reciting the Gettysburg Address for the first time. "Forty-or-so" and "Sixty-ish" are clueless. "As-old-as-twenty-five" understands English and begins to confab with the other two in Italian. Sabrina had told me the seventh floor.

After the continuing confab of the three magi at the desk, I'm sent to the fifth floor. I am not certain exactly why, but everyone agrees I must go to the fifth floor.

The elevator is tiny. The woefully out of date inspection sticker indicates the capacity for this car is "Cinque Personne." There were eight of us from floors zero to four. I know now why the Sicilian national dish is "Pasta con Sarde." We are packed like sardines. All we need is the Florio label printed on the elevator door.

By the fourth floor, I'm freed from the "Sardine Can." I'm met by three women the approximate age-range of the magi at the desk downstairs who sent me to the fifth floor. These three women, more muses than magi, are not nearly so conventionally attired as the men. None of them is in any way beautiful (rare in a city where almost everyone is good-looking). But if they were graded on effort, they would each get an A.

"Donna 40-or-so", in a black leotard and a grey knit dress that simply will not stay below the appropriate areas of her anatomy for optimum respectability, is wearing four-inch, bejeweled, platform pumps. Her hair is a color somewhere between copper and orange—a color to be found nowhere in nature or on any PMS chip. Her cosmetics rather artfully accent her hair. She tugs hopelessly to pull the grey knit dress over her privates, while wobbling precariously on the bejeweled pumps. She is undoubtedly one of the great architectural wonders of Palermo.

"Donna 25-at-most" is more simply dressed. She is showing her two more senior colleagues a picture of her two French bulldogs Tandre and Sandre on her telephone. I have to see "due beddae," and we all four ooh and aah over the pups.

After nearly ten minutes, "Donna Sixty-ish" asks me my business. Whereupon, all of what I thought was an understanding of English on her part while we admired the "due beddae" has disappeared. No one understands who Mr. Enzo is or know anything about a meeting. So I sit down at the desk of Signor Cossenza and the three muses disappear.

Signor Cossenza appears and he is every bit as dumbfounded by the presence of this American in his office as the magi and the muses. He quickly moves from puzzled to hospitable and introduces himself. I do the same. He tells me he speaks no English. I tell him I understand a bit of Italian. Then he launches into a full-blown, high-speed discussion of something, the meaning of which I am likely never to retrieve from memories of things past.

After maybe ten or so more minutes of pleasantries, Signor Cossenza determines that he and I have no business with one another and sends me to the elevator where I determine that I will head to the seventh floor where Sabrina told me to go in the first place.

The elevator door opens and another figure whom I take for a security officer nabs me and pulls me into the crowded elevator car. He launches into a long explanation of something, none of which I understand. We get off on the seventh floor. He leads me to an office where he tells me to be seated. I sit and see a nameplate on his desk: "Viscenzo Cirri." This is Mr. Enzo.

Finalmente!

After four more people wander into his office at various times, the meeting begins. I state my case. We talk for nearly two hours. Final verdict: My project will only be eligible to receive regional or European Union funds if I have a Sicilian partner. They all wish me well and send me on my way.

In our interview with Leoluca Orlando, Mayor of Palermo, he tells me, "All the people who came in Sicily became Sicilians." After my meeting with Mr. Enzo, I'm certain that I've become Sicilian.

Walking back to Giuseppe's after my meeting, I see a dog run near the Giardini Inglese where people bring puppies and kittens for adoption. Sicilians have pets and Sicilians are avid walkers. And when they walk, they are often walking their dogs. On Via Della Libertà, I meet many Jack Russell terriers and dachshunds.

In Palermo, I notice two canine social classes. There are what I would call "market dogs," and their higher-rent counterparts that I've dubbed "boulevard dogs."

Market dogs are generally big mixed breeds. They are mostly old and very fat. They look rough and seem to be in a continual state of slumber around the market stalls of Vucciria, Ballaro, or Borgo Vecchio. Market dogs have none of the perkiness of the spoiled and much-poofed boulevard doggies.

When it comes to cats, I assume there are boulevard felines. But you never see them. They are likely declawed and live in the many high-rise condominium buildings lining the Via Della Libertà.

Market cats only show themselves at certain times of the day. They are as circumspect as spies and they have as much distrust in their eyes as New York City rats.

Market cats are feral kitties. They are nearly everywhere in Sicily. In the early mornings and at market, cats are reconnoitering the palatial and rundown, the weeds and gardens, the swanky shops and the humble market stalls.

These feline funambulists skulk along the roof lines of churches and palazzi that are world monuments to Baroque or Liberty architecture. Nestled below street-corner religious shrines, mother market cats suckle their litters on walkways in markets crusted in grime dating back to the Counter Reformation.

Above: Giovanni Falcone, Anti-Mafia prosecutor
Below: Paolo Borsellino, Anti-Mafia prosecutor

EIGHT

*As an Italian, I have little problem reconciling violence
with culture.*

—Camille Paglia from Sexual Personae

The Fiaccolota is a yearly candlelight procession honoring
the memories of Giovanni Falcone and Paolo Borsellino,
two heroic prosecutors assassinated by the Mafia in 1992.
They had been extraordinarily successful in bringing Mafiosi
to justice, and they paid for their successes with their lives.
In December of 1987, at the end of the two-year juridical
proceedings known in Sicily as the maxi-trial, three-hundred
and sixty of four-hundred and seventy-four organized crime
defendants were convicted of offenses that included one-
hundred and twenty murders, drug trafficking, and extortion.

Falcone and Borsellino received invaluable testimony
from Tomasso Buscetta, the highest-level Sicilian organized
crime boss to turn "pentito," or informant. Buscetta did what
no other Mafioso had done: He revealed the structure of La
Cosa Nostra, its internal workings and the extent to which it
had penetrated "legitimate" businesses and politics. The maxi-
trial verdicts struck the strongest blow that Italian authorities
have ever delivered to organized crime in Sicily. For this
unprecedented success, Falcone and Borsellino died violent
deaths, the former killed, along with his wife and bodyguards,

when Mafia assassins blew up a stretch of highway as his motorcade traveled from the Palermo airport. The latter was killed by a car bomb outside his mother's house.

Speaking about crime in Sicily, one judge coined the term, "collective criminality." Any discussion of "collective criminality" cannot be vague or euphemistic, which might contribute to a romanticizing of criminal acts. I have no intention of making a film that participates in the romanticized mythology created by novelists and Hollywood fifilmmakers. "Collective criminality" is not a movie. It is real crime, perpetrated against real people, frequently by members of their own communities and sometimes by members of their own families. These crimes continue to inflict severe and enduring damage on the economy, ecology, and the very soul of Sicily.

The Catholic Church seldom spoke out against collective criminality in Sicily. In fact, the Church too often has either turned a blind eye to the Mafia's crimes or, shockingly, condoned them on the grounds that so-called "men of honor" deserved the sacraments as much as anyone else. (During the Cold War, the fact that Mafiosi were fervent anti-Communists contributed to the Church's indulgent attitude.) In the 1950s Cardinal Ruffini openly campaigned for Mafia-backed politicians who were also members of Democrazia Cristiana (the Christian Democratic Party).

In the 1970s, Sicilian criminals were flush with heroin money. Competition in the drug trade was fierce, resulting in major crime wars on the island. During the 1980s, conflicts between Mafiosi from Corleone and older Palermo clans escalated into previously unheard-of levels of atrocious violence as Mafiosi slaughtered each other, the police, and the prosecutors. Through all this, the Church either remained silent or offered at best pro-forma denunciations of violence. Grassroots anti-Mafia clergy begged the hierarchy to forcefully and unequivocally condemn the Mafia as evil and anti-Christian.

In 1993, after the deaths of Falcone and Borsellino, Pope John Paul II heard the priests' entreaties and in a speech in Agrigento condemned Sicilian organized crime. His words were met with repercussion. The Mafiosi blew up a church and murdered an anti-Mafia priest.

Today, a new Sicily is emerging. In Palermo young activists fed up with the Mafia and its parasitic presence in the country's economic life have formed Addiopizzo, a movement that encourages local businesses to refuse to pay the pizzo, or "protection" money. (The name "Addiopizzo" means "So Long Protection Payment.") Addiopizzo has enlisted hundreds of businesses in Palermo and has spread to Catania, the island's second city. The movement cannot defeat the Mafia by itself, but its emergence signifies a growing resistance to organized crime, particularly among Sicily's young people.

Sicily is changing in other ways. Although the island has a reputation for conservative sexual morality and stifling "family values," in 2012 Sicilian voters elected their first openly gay governor, Rosario Crocetta, a former communist who served two terms as the mayor of the Mafia-infested town of Gela. As governor, Crocetta has vowed to continue the anti-Mafia campaign he launched in Gela.

Sicilian business is changing as well, becoming more modern and transparent. In 2011 Confindustria, Italy's main private employers' association, expelled more than thirty businessmen from its Sicilian chapter for failing to report Mafia extortionists. Confindustria only takes such action when it is certain that individual businessmen or entire enterprises are colluding with the Mafia's protection rackets or with organized crime in general.

Sicily is changing in many ways, defying old stereotypes and myths. We are now seeing glimpses of these transformations in Sicilian life. We are seeing a few new and surprising realities that contradict perceived ideas and outdated images.

Leonardo Sciascia's book *The Day of the Owl* demonstrates how organized crime manages to sustain itself in the face of the anomie inherent in Sicilian life.

Who is Anti-fascist, Anti-Communist, or Anti-crime? Sometimes, it's hard to tell.

While incarcerated in a United States prison, gangster Lucky Luciano was said to have provided intelligence to the Allied Forces for their landing in Sicily. Luciano's release from prison was part of the bargain.

When they entered a Sicilian town, Allied Forces immediately dissolved the local Fascist government and frequently asked local clergy to recommend a respected individual in the town to act as interim mayor. Too often, a local crime box received the appointment.

As I write this, it is the twentieth-anniversary commemoration of Falcone's and Borsellino's deaths, a reminder that resistance to Mafia crime in Sicily must continue. Of course, the Mafia will adapt to the changing landscape to create a livelihood. Perhaps they will move to activities that leave individuals and small business people alone.

Many Sicilians simply cannot see that their future is in their own hands. And many have left the island nation because of barriers. It's time to remove those barriers in Sicily. The Mafia is not the only barrier, but it is the most important one. If the Sicilian people are strong and intelligent enough to end the Mafia as a barrier to social and economic mobility, then the rest of the barriers will be easier to remove.

In the Sicilian past, nearly every imposition of order – from invaders, nobility, the Church, or crime bosses—was a thinly veiled excuse to extort from the Sicilian people. "Order" is not to be trusted, they believe. It is too Anglo-Saxon. This phobia is extremely challenging to that part of me that is American and, therefore, more English than anything else.

As Americans, we assume fair play. This is the archetype of the naïve American. Yet, we not only believe in fair play, we stand our ground for it. Many Europeans look on us as fools for such behavior. But such behaviors have proven extremely successful for us and fatal for the likes of Falcone and Borsellino.

Salvatore "Toto" Riina (1939-2017) was the head of the Sicilian Mafia. He was known for a ruthless murder campaign that reached its peak in the early 1990s with Falcone's and Borsellino's assassinations. It was said that he drank champagne when he was informed of Falcone's death. This is the quintessential Sicilian drama because Riina was replete in his villainy. He was a monster, not simply a man of many sins like the rest of us. Attributing to Riina qualities beyond those of a man make him something closer to a character out of Homer.

This kind of representation in the media, whether through film, the press, or fictional literature, is utterly wrong-headed. Those criminals are and were men, not gods. Mythologizing them strengthens their powers of illusion and influence.

The Irish mother of a high school friend would often extol the gentility and grandfatherly qualities of a local crime boss who I knew to have murdered members of his own family. I failed to see the gentility in the man. Adoring the falseness in his persona has an ironic aura that remains ugly and powerful.

My friend's mother's dramatization of the man in some ways sanctified him. He became a saint or exterminating angel who did the needful work of God himself. In such a story lives Sicily's great flaw, a flaw not unlike Ireland's. Both, I believe, are rooted in Catholicism.

NINE

He who is silent and bows his head dies every time he does so.
He who speaks aloud and walks with his head held high
dies only once.

—Giovanni Falcone

What is the meaning of manhood in Sicily? Or, for that matter, anywhere? Is a man the dignified, dark-hearted Prince Fabrizio from Giuseppe Tomasi di Lampedusa's novel The Leopard (Il Gattopardo)? Is manhood defined by being a crime boss or fisherman or carter? Who is a man of "honor?" Is he a father, a member of the clergy, a magistrate, or a man who loves other men?

There is an almost rabid pride in Sicilians in upholding family name and reputation.

Sicilians love their family. They love family life. Sicilians love their mothers. In fact, the mother is the center of the universe for Sicilians. The two greatest images in religious life of Sicily are the mother, and then the other is the child. Sicilians think of Christ as a baby, the child Christ. All Sicilian mothers eventually assume the aspect of the sorrowful mother of Christ.

— Gaetano Cipolla, Sicilian-American Author and Scholar

There can be no discussion of the far-reaching and varied influences on Sicilian society without addressing the issue of crime.

In the story of Sicily, gangsters are the identified villains. And, grant you, they are no doubt villains. They are not the only villains, however, and at the heart of things not the worst villains. My documentary film *Sicily: Land of Love and Strife* creates several moments when an astute viewer will come to see this truth, without ever deviating from its mission to tell the story in a very elegant manner.

In Blood Brotherhoods: The Rise of the Italian Mafias, author and historian John Dickie, writes, "For decades the Bourbons recruited their police from among the city's most feared criminals." He goes on to discuss the "co-management" of crime where, in Sicily and Southern Italy, criminals colluded with crime fighters from the period of Risorgimento (1815-1871) to the present day on behalf of the interests of both groups and at the expense of the Italian people.

Dozens of sources have discussed the deal made with Lucky Luciano during World War II as the Allies were invading Sicily.

"Power is power," my father would say. He believed that every solution was brokered—that law enforcement did business with criminals; that legitimate governments negotiated with terrorists; and that religious institutions, in the interests of their leadership, would wheel and deal with the same blind eye to the law.

In Italy's Commedia dell'arte, a character in performance might be killed in a fight and fall dramatically dead on the stage. A few moments later, the same player would jump to his feet revived from death and share, through some manner of wink to his audience, the jibe that implies, "Oh, come on, folks, this is just a play."

But a room splattered like a Jackson Pollock painting in human blood and millions of tiny globs of flesh is no comedy.

Especially when the victim of three gunblasts, pumped at close range from a twelve-gauge into the viscera was a member of your family. How might I convince you, my reader, that the violence of war and crime is real?

No group considering themselves legitimate can resolve their problems through murder. Nor can any group blind itself to economic opportunity for all that has been denied to previous generations and will likely be denied to those that follow. The medievalism of Mafia thinking is as obsolete a struggle for the Mafia as it is for the rest of us. We are all, in fact, on the same side. We cannot continue to poison the body of someone's child with drugs and think we are not poisoning our own children with the burden of a drug culture. This applies to the pollution of land with hazardous waste, the sex trade, and even the stealing of the bare necessities from countless numbers of children because of the gambling addictions of their parents. These burdens are placed on all of us. It is time for many individuals to come to their collective senses.

These are not victimless crimes. The perpetrators harm themselves and their children and grandchildren. We must not give these sects, or whatever they are, room to breathe. Arrest them, bring them to justice. We must refocus on these elements in society.

Sicilian or not, crime is crime. We must never give these elements a home. I refuse to glamorize in any way the destructive behaviors of organized crime. Such activities do not amount to any form of a valuable life well-lived.

As I have seen first-hand, trying at the end of life to buy into respectability, or into heaven, is vain and pathetic. That's not what it means to be a man and certainly not a man of honor. These crimes and the people who commit them, by no means represent what it means to be Sicilian.

This is not a movie. This is something we confront every day, so sometimes people forget that Sicilian are mostly the victims of the Mafia.

—Katia Amore, Magazine Editor and Teacher

Organized crime is not the stuff of scenes imagined by Francis Ford Coppola and Martin Scorsese. Organized crime is not "pretend." And it looks nothing like scenes performed by Brando or Di Niro. Think of the people you love most. Think of them killed, maimed, robbed of their economic security by other very real people. That is organized crime.

When we speak of the art, the architecture, the landscape of Sicily, we begin to enter a world of mythology or dreams. This is crucial to some kinds of storytelling. But in the discussion of organized crime, I want no myths, no dreams, no heroics. I want only real people, real death, real theft, a genuine highjacking of the economic futures of generations past, present, and those possibly to come.

Many women have shown leadership in the fight to end the Mafia. I believe women are key players in this struggle toward ending organized crime. Women are the creators of family and strongly influence the ideas we have about family and home life.

In recent times, Mafia wives and daughters have turned state's evidence.

"These are the examples of real female liberation," says Dr. Ombretta Ingrasci who has written widely on Mafia wives and women's lives in modern Italy. "By turning state's evidence, they reject the male-dominated Mafia system."

Sicily succeeded in the Agricultural Revolution, sold citrus fruits to all the sailors of the world to travel around without scurvy, and then Britain and France had an Industrial Revolution and Sicily didn't. So Sicily stopped in time and got left behind and that was when Sicily ceased to be the center of the world.

—Veronica Hughes Di Grigoli, Author and Sicily Blogger

It is a complicated era, because it is an era when Sicily is considered something of a backwater by the ruling power of Spain.

—Andrew Edwards, Author and Scholar

You had all kinds of power in the revolution to sweep away your criminal record, kill your enemies with impunity, grab hold of some land, and make sure the courts did your bidding. So it is really from that revolutionary moment in the early to mid Nineteenth Century that the Sicilian Mafia, the sect, the police at the time called it a sect, that this sect emerged. The Mafia is a kind of freemasonry for criminals. Let's get it straight what it is. It is a secret society modeled on the Free Masons. Now the Free Masons are a perfectly reputable organization, but their way of organizing themselves was effectively stolen by the worst criminals in Sicily.

—John Dickie, Author and Scholar

Dickie calls the Mafia "a secret society," but I don't completely agree. The Mafia is not secret. In both the Kansas City of my childhood and present-day Sicily, the Mafia functions right out in the open and is as much a secret as most extramarital love affairs. In Kansas City, people knew. They just didn't talk about it. Today, we talk openly about everything.

Just because we may speak in a whisper does not make something a secret. I suspect the Mafia wants people to know their exploits. I've known some who talked up Mafia exploits, even exaggerated them.

These days, the Mafia seems somewhat ham-fisted to me. That doesn't mean they are ineffective. In my experience, very few of these guys were any sort of geniuses. Most seemed lacking in stealth and observation skills. And when your only tool is a hammer, you see all your problems as nails.

The Mafia still exists. They still succeed, but their time has come. They are a living anachronism pushed into the modern world. They know it. The young people know it. The mafiosi of Sicily have outlived their credibility.

I believe there will be a day when there is a Sicily without the Mafia and an Italy without the religious domination of the Church. It will be a very great day indeed for both nations.

Three Spanish knights, they were brothers in the dim and distant past, took refuge on the island because they had murdered a nobleman who had raped their sister. And for taking this blood revenge, they had to flee and go into exile, and they went into exile on Favignana. And the story goes that they spent nine years or twenty-one years making up the rules of the honored society on this island. In Sicily they call it Sicilianismo. Sicilianism, this idea of the sort of irreducible peculiarity of the Sicilian character, of Sicilian identity. Sicilianismo, in a sense, I am afraid has also often been a tool of the Mafia. The Mafia has an ideology, has people who are prepared to spread misconceptions on its behalf, its lawyers, its politicians, and they've often been the ones who've been arguing, you do not understand us. The Mafia is not a

*product of Sicilians' love of their family. It is quite the contrary.
Sicilian mafiosi, who are already being defined very early in their
history as middle-class criminals, upwardly mobile criminals, they
want to pass their wealth and their power onto their children. Just
as importantly, they wanted to forge marriage alliances with other
bosses within the sect.*

—John Dickie, Author and Scholar

These people are like the Taliban. There is nothing fun about them.

—Katia Amore, Magazine Editor and Teacher

*The Mafia has territorial control in some areas of the large cities.
Where there is no work, there is widespread urban decay. And the
youth who grew up in these neighborhoods are easy prey for those
who manage the drug trafficking.*

—Edoardo Zaffuto, Anti-Mafia Activist

*Mafia will ignore you until you bring money. When Mafia smells
money, Mafia will be knocking at your door.*

—Giovanni Gallo, University Professor

*People are realizing that it is necessary to do something to change
to refuse to pay, to say no to the Mafia. And now even in Palermo,
it is possible to tour the city just going to this organization called
Addiopizzo which unites all the businessmen and all the activities
all stay away from paying protection money and report criminals to the police. I am one of the members of the organization,
non-profit organization Addiopizzo. We organize Mafia-free tours
for students who want to know what Sicily really is. The phenom-*

enon protection money is still very strong. The police have been dismantling the Pizzo system, the Pizzo network.

—Edoardo Zaffuto, Anti-Mafia Activist

It is important that every Sicilian citizen takes a stand against the big issue affecting Sicilians that is the Mafia, organized crime.

—Rosario Lupo, Anti-Mafia Activist

I am proud to be the mayor of Palermo where a priest, a Catholic priest...was killed by the Mafia in 1993 and now is recognized like a saint...and I am proud to be the mayor of the city where this priest was born, and close friend of mine was killed by the Mafia after so many years of priest and bishops being friends of mafiosos.

—Leoluca Orlando, Mayor of Palermo

Rosario Lupo, Anti-Mafia activist and the author

TEN

Whatever, in fact, is modern in our life we owe to the Greeks.
Whatever is an anachronism is due to medievalism.

—Oscar Wilde, The Critic as Artist

Sicily is a fish. She is not a fish that I eat. She is a fish that eats me. More to the point, she swallows me whole. In the States, Sicily is for me a preoccupation. In Sicily, Sicily is my total occupation. She will suffer no rivals.

I have been swallowed. I am engulfed by her dark feminine waters, her rugged earth, her shimmering beauty.

Nature, as ephemeral as the lemon blossom or as enduring as Etna, is what we hold fast, what we save within ourselves to remind us why we continue, to remind us that there is promise, that the future has some worth.

The market is chaos. Everyone is loading and unloading, buying, selling, packaging, walking, smoking, complaining, and ignoring everything, even what they seem to be doing.

Peach season is nearly over. Most of the peaches in the market are brown and going soft. The remaining peaches reek of a sweet-sick stench of rot. A puffy-handed strega nonna in a stained apron, cuts the seeds from the rotting fruits, dropping them into an ancient caldron where she simmers her mushy harvest into jam. This is more alchemy than we humans may deserve.

Another woman tips a boy to carry a lug of the rotting peaches for her. I want to follow them home. I am immensely curious as to what she is going to do with them. I want to watch her cook whatever concoction she is planning and then, of course, taste it when it is finished.

At Quattro Canti, I cross to a corner where the horse-drawn carriages wait for fares. This area of the street is rife with the odor of horse piss. A driver and his carriage wait at the Statue of the Genius of Palermo. Quattro Canti is a remarkably designed Baroque architectural configuration intersecting two of Palermo's major thoroughfares. It is a place where sheer elegance and utter dross easily coexist. This is inescapably Sicily. This is the Sicily I love.

Today I sit on a low stone wall in the Valley of the Temples in Agrigento. The ruins, the mountainside, the sea. The wind landward carries the thinnest whiff of skunk. I have forgotten the batteries for my camera. The gods have given me a day off. I pay tribute to those gods today and will return tomorrow for photographs. How lucky can I be? Domani!

The land is rocky and uneven. Some very old olive trees have thick, knotted trunks. Their bark seems as timeworn as the stones of the temples while the variegated grey-greens of the leaves and olives make them as alive as this moment. The trunks are not solid. There are open spaces in them, spaces you can see through.

As I scribble about olive trees, an ant drops onto my notebook. I look from the tiny crawler to individual stones, pieces of the Temple of Zeus that are bigger than I could have imagined. Placing them must have required aid from the hand of Zeus himself.

I climb these rocks like my forbearers, like a Capricorn, the goat of my astrological sign. My feet not nearly so sure as they once were, despite the fact I am becoming an old goat on an ancient Sicilian hillside writing, now, in the shadow of the Temple of Concordia.

At each shrine, I pay homage in turn to Demeter, Hades, Zeus, Poseidon, Aphrodite, Apollo, and Persephone.

Like a Buddhist, I walk in a circle around each of the temples as a meditation. I walk to the left —a sinestra because being gay is like being left-handed: sinister in Sicily. Non-Roman Catholic Italians were called "lefties" or "left-handed dagos." They were thought to be "other than." A pretense or aspiration to another station in life was left-handed. Hence, mia omogia sinestra.

At Persephone's shrine, I encircle her temple twice. She is the patroness of Sicily and to her I dedicate my work.

Paganism is so much more appealing to me because it's dead. Possibly Christianity would have some appeal if it understood it was in its death throes.

I sit again to rest. I am surrounded by ragged broom plants on a barren hillside. Ants have decided it is lunchtime and I'm lunch. Three crows fly circles around the Temple of Hera, then wider out over the entire valley. I take this to be a good omen but wonder which deity is responsible for insect repellent. I'm guessing that would be Aphrodite because the swarming of insects resonates with desire. Possibly her son Eros because tiny arrows are darting and pinching at me, then they're gone.

As author and Sicilian-American storyteller Gioia Timpanelli tells us, "Eros was male and female, female and male. Eros was one, and almost nothing can be done without Eros, without that love of beauty, form, and the spontaneous appearance."

It must be Eros. I am being eaten alive.

ELEVEN

*It is everywhere, it is identical, and it is palpable. These men have
fallen from their ideals. In virtue of a vast and hypocritical system
of commerce they amass wealth and power, defend it with mean
intrigue and violent assault, blunt their moral sense
in pursuit of more, relax into sensuality and are lifted
to arrogance. It is time that they have a severe lesson.*

—Joseph McCabe

The world of my childhood was, for me, a long captivity.
In the storytelling of my neighborhood, school, and
family, hindsight provides enchantment that did not exist.
Where I grew up, real life was boring. We were intellectually
malnourished, and I was weak from it.

Abandoned by his own father, my father was a victim
of violent abuse at the hands of his uncles. It made him an
angry, violent man who exercised little or no control over
his outbursts when dealing with small children and his
remarkably passive wife. Angry outbursts kept my father's
concerns central to our household. Only his needs filled the
air in our tiny apartment. There was room for little else. I
wanted to escape very badly.

I was in continual pursuit of what other people knew. I
wanted to know the secrets to their seemingly happy lives. I got
to know many people. I had a reputation for gregariousness. In

a life dominated by the neighborhood and the church, meeting people, going places, seeing things was my quest. I welcomed any opportunity for escape from such a repressive environment.

What passed for success in the milieu of my upbringing didn't appeal to me at all. All roads led to marriage, family, business careers, and the church. It was all so mediocre. I suffered from the mistaken notion that a Jesuit high school way across town would change things for me.

The American Catholic Church of my upbringing was an Irish church. The Jesuits from the Midwestern boys' high school I attended were mostly Irish and German. The paradigm, though, was intensely Irish. Kansas City, or the old Kansas City anyway, was an Irish town. These Irishmen of the Society of Jesus had given their lives to the Society. Most of them had been recruited into the order before they truly understood what they were getting into or giving up. Many of them understood little of real life. Grown men without lives, without sanctioned or acknowledged sexual outlets, and with less understanding of risk and responsibility than the mostly affluent teenagers they taught—these were the Jesuits who tried to teach me.

It worked until it no longer worked. There was a point in my life when I forced myself upon those around me and eventually made people fear and even hate me. It wasn't just my anger that provoked these reactions. It was my young gay man's pretensions, always dressing down my elders. I took the moral high ground with a stridency that can only be produced by a Jesuit education. The Jesuits I knew certainly had mediocre minds, and the ample amounts of whiskey they consumed didn't help. But they did have wickedly sharp tongues, a trait often found among adherents of the love that, in those days, didn't dare speak its name. To me, "alcoholic," "queer" and "Jesuit" were as indissolubly linked as the Father, the Son, and the Holy Ghost.

I wanted none of the girls I knew. Some were friends, but I had no desire for any of them. My male friends were the center of my world.

My early teens to early twenties consisted of many an attempted jail-break from the prison of words built around me by Jesuits. Sex was a great revelation. The Irish had infected me with too much language—and also with their Jansenism, which exalts the spirit and denigrates the body—and not enough of the earth. My body and the bodies of others became my connections to the planet, my conversation with the universe. This is matter-of-fact eroticism that is evident in Sicilians both in Sicily and the United States.

The most spiritual aspect of sex is its utter escape from the tyranny of the spiritual, from the mysticism that distances us from the earth and our senses, those essential sources of learning and understanding. Through sex, my notion of the spiritual was shattered. Earth and sky were broken apart like a seed pod. I began to breathe as an adult. I understood that I am an animal and part of the planet, not separated from it. Only then did compassion begin to take hold of me. I was becoming human, no longer the angel of righteousness or a quick-witted, badmouth dark-angel fulminating like Hermes the god of words who, like me, was a second son.

My Aunt Kathryn referred to the Mafiosi in our town as "malandrini." The word translates as something close to rogues or bullies. Gay people and Sicilians have something in common. Both groups have been bullied for far too long.

To be bullied is to deny the reality of it. It is human to escape helplessness, to go to another place where you're powerful, in control. Most often that "other place," that haven or hideout, is a place within the mind. That place is invented, a place of imagination. Imagination, invention, and creativity are often associated with gay people and Sicilians, and I am both.

I know a good bit about exiting my existence by journeying deeper into a world of imagination. As a very young man, I did this with music and books. I created an interior life that was by far more real to me than the tangible one in which I lived.

Sartre tells us that such flights make us actors in the world we have departed. This is how he described the French novelist and playwright Jean Genet. The child Genet, forced into a life of denial of himself as thief and homosexual, emerges living an imagined self, carrying within him the stifled self he was. To some degree, this is true of each of us, but for Genet it was an extreme situation that brought forth the wildest of literary inventions.

The bullied and the stifled are actors impersonating someone all the time, even if the ones we're impersonating are ourselves. Like Buddhists, we know the thinness of self.

People like me envision grandeur as few others ever could. This sense of stateliness is embodied deeply in the contrasting aspects of Sicily. I love Sicily because it is both halves of me: the enshrined grandeur and the bullied, suffocated child. Calling this anything but sad is a lie.

Genuine sadness is not the least self-indulgent. Sadness is a true internal division between what is and what might have been. Sadness is the process of bringing the two together under the same tent. Gays no longer want to be considered sad. Gays and lesbians are all upbeat and positive, but that may very well be the falsest of poses.

Young gays and lesbians are still committing suicide over bullying. The sadness is not gone. These are young people who very likely could be good and devoted friends to the very people who are bullying them. These bullied young people likely imagine a life where they are included, where they are part of the mix. That they are not, that they die for it, is nothing but sad. Every news story of a bullied young person who has committed suicide brings back every memory I have of being bullied, of being told through word and deed that I was excluded because something about me was horrific, unacceptable, not to be trusted.

By the same token, how can Sicilians not be sad about so much of what has transpired in their land? There's no way forward by denying the sadness. For most of us, it is the only way forward.

Nineteenth-Century Taormina was the resort for all the gay German barons.

—Giovanni Gallo, University Professor

Word got around in Europe about this kind of paradise. It ultimately became a kind of European fire island and European men of means started coming there.

—Charles Leslie, Author and Art Collector

Lots of these homosexual writers had been in the south of France, and were looking for somewhere new to go and they found their inspiration in Greek Sicily. The lifestyle, way of life, was acceptable by the locals.

—Suzanne and Andrew Edwards, Authors

The Sicilians still, to this day, live a lot closer to the earth than the rest of Italians and the rest of Europe, surely.

—Charles Leslie, Author and Art Collector

At one point in the community forum in this department, some student brought up this issue, Professor X is gay. And I remember very presently that all the other students answered, who cares?

—Giovanni Gallo, University Professor, Catania

I had a very easy time coming out to my family. My parents told me they understood a long time ago and were waiting for me to tell them. It wasn't a problem. For other young people, this is a much greater problem in their lives. Many of my friends cannot come out to their families.

—Mirko Pace, Sicilian LGBT Activist

People in the LGBT community can be out, and live their life in a reasonable way. I won't say freely but in a reasonable degree of freedom, all in big cities.

—Giovanni Gallo

They are not alone. Beyond their teachers, schools, and schoolmates, there is a world of young people like them with the same issues.

—Daniela Tomasino, Sicilian LGBT Activist

You move from the country to the big city and you are free, but if you go back to the small town, you are sort of put back in your closet, clothes, and protect yourself.

—Giovanni Gallo

The title of my film and this book come from a quote from Empedocles: I will tell a double story...at one time all coming together into one by Love and at another being borne apart by hatred of Strife.

Many myths and stories surround Empedocles. He was known for his brilliant oratory, his knowledge of nature, and near-magical powers. He was a philosopher, a poet, and something of a shaman. He was also a homosexual.

Like Pythagoras, Empedocles believed in the transmigration of the soul—that souls can be reincarnated between humans, animals, and even plants.

Diogenes Laërtius tells the story of Empedocles dying by throwing himself into the volcano at Mount Etna so people would believe he had vanished into thin air and transformed into a god. Diogenes goes on to say that the volcano threw back one of his sandals, revealing his suicidal deception.

Another legend has it that Empedocles threw himself in the volcano to prove to his disciples that he was immortal. He believed he would come back as a god among men after being devoured by the fire.

TWELVE

By the year 1100, when the superb Arab cities of
Spain and Sicily were at the height of their
splendour, when the Normans had embraced alike
the culture and the scepticism of the Arabs, Rome
had sunk back into semi-barbarism.

—Joseph McCabe

Sicilians have had at last count, and you can count more,
maybe seventeen or eighteen different invasions of the island.

— Gaetano Cipolla, Sicilian-American Author and Scholar

This is a people which has been subdued, the Greeks and the Car-
thaginians. Sicily was the first province of the Roman Empire. As
you go on through history we then talk of various other people, so
we have the Byzantines then the Arabs for a long period. And then,
incredibly, the Normans in 1061. Then after we have various
French overlords, Spanish domination, various kinds of Spanish,
the Aragonese, the Catalans, and eventually the Germans. There
are even some Sicilians who regard the Garibaldis landing, he
came to reunite the whole of Italy. They regarded this as the last
invasion, the Piedmontese invasion.

—Joseph Farrell, Author and Sicilian Scholar

Sicilians are suspicious of anybody who comes because everybody who has come to Sicily, has come not to give it something, has come to take something from it.

—Gaetano Cipolla

Twenty-seven centuries ago, there was not far away from where we are right now, the first Greek settlement. And Greek have brought a lot of new ideas, philosophy, art, this new sense of beauty as well.

— Carmelo Giafriddu, Geologist and Etna Expert

The Greeks came here because they had nothing to eat in Greece. They came to Sicily and found all the elements just right for establishing the greater Greece, and we became a part of it.

—Giuseppe Li Rosi, producer of ancient strains of Sicilian wheat

And it wasn't only a one-way street from Greece to Sicily. Sicily contributed a great deal to Greek civilization as well. 2,500 years ago, Sicily had navigable rivers all over, and the forests, the forests were growing all over the place. Now if you go in the center of Sicily, you see a lunar landscape. When the Romans came, they took out all the trees. They deforested the whole island so that they could plant their wheat and make Sicily the granary of Rome to feed their armies.

— Gaetano Cipolla

For centuries, Sicily was a launchpad of culture throughout Europe. The North Africans brought their culture here. The Vikings came here. The Arabs came here.

—Veronica Hughes Di Grigoli, Author and Sicily Blogger

The geographical position of Sicily is decisive, Giuseppe Antonio Borgese is a Sicilian himself. He defines Sicily as being an island which is not island enough.

—Joseph Farrell

You have to understand Sicily's history, and the single most important thing you need to understand is that throughout most of its history Sicily was not an outpost. Sicily was the center of the world.

—Veronica Hughes Di Grigoli

King Roger I was born in Normandy in 1040 CE. He was descended from Viking invaders of what is now the coast of France. A newcomer to Christianity, Roger I wanted to impress the Pope with his fervor by invading Muslim Sicily. In 1071 CE, he fought to take control of the island, which had been held for nearly two-hundred years by various North African and Arabic Muslims. By 1090, Roger I ruled the entire island and a good portion of the southern Italian peninsula.

This was significant because, for the first time in history, Sicily had become a nation. Roger I reigned until his death in 1101 CE at which time his twelve-year-old son was crowned Roger II. Thus began what was to be Sicily's true golden age.

Roger II has been called "the half-heathen king" and "the baptized Sultan of Sicily." His father may have conquered the island, but Muslim ideas had, nonetheless, conquered Roger II. His court boasted a diverse collection of philosophers, mathematicians, doctors, geographers and poets with no superiors in Europe, and in whose company Roger II spent much of his time.

King Roger II was fascinated by geography and scientific inquiry, ideas brought to his court by the Muslims in Sicily. He surrounded himself with Jewish, Muslim, and Christian scholars and delighted in their philosophical debate.

Under the supervision of al-Idrisi, one of Roger II's chief Arab Muslim advisors, the king commissioned the most accurate and comprehensive map of the known world at that time.

With considerable Muslim and Jewish participation in his government, Roger II ruled over a dynamic culture and a booming economy. His kingdom was unlike anything else in Europe during the Dark Ages.

Among the many great innovations that the Muslim Arabs brought to Sicily, one of the greatest would have to be irrigation systems. For the first time in its history, Sicily began to live up to its agricultural potential, becoming the breadbasket of the region. Muslim Arabs also introduced new crops including oranges, lemons, cotton, date palms, and rice.

During his reign, Roger II commissioned the construction of the Cappella Palatina, the royal chapel for the Sicilian Norman palace. The tiny jewel box of a church is a blend of both Muslim and Byzantine influences. I love this chapel because it so clearly attests to the exuberant cultural influences at work in King Roger's court.

Some historians suggest that medieval times were Europe's Dark Ages. This bit of eurocentrism ignores the many achievements from the Arab and Byzantine worlds that came into contact with Norman Sicily. The arts and scholarship flourished in ways unknown in northern and central Europe at that time. Palermo assumed its place as a center of learning and expression alongside Cordoba, Byzantium, Alexandria, and Baghdad.

Until about 1000 or 1050 C.E., Greek, Latin, and Arabic were spoken in Sicily. The Sicilian language was used at court and was the poetic language. And it was used as the language of poetry throughout Italy. "The very Italian language," wrote Arthur Stanley Riggs, "as Dante himself acknowledges, had its feeble beginnings in the court of the Emperor Frederick II at Palermo."

Sicily has its own language. Naples has its own language, Venice has its own language. They are not dialects. They are not corruptions of Italian, because Italian came later. When Sicily became Italian in 1861, there were so many people who were—well, ninety-five percent of the people, ninety percent of the people—were illiterate. That means they didn't know how to read or write. Did they know Italian? Of course not. Did anybody know Italian in 1871? Maybe three percent of the whole population of Italy understood Tuscan in 1871, three percent!

— Gaetano Cipolla, Sicilian-American Author and Scholar

Sicily up till that point was a very cosmopolitan society. They had Greeks who spoke the Greek language and they had their own legal system and their own way of dressing and their own professions, and then they had the Muslims from North Africa with their own Sharia law and then they had the Jews—who were the scribes and the interpreters who had their own legal system, their own language, their own schools—and they all lived together. Along came the Spanish with the Inquisition, and that wasn't allowed anymore. And everyone had to be a Catholic according to the rules that the Spanish imposed, or be put to death. So lots of people fled, and that was when Sicily became a monoculture. And to me, that was the end of the glory days of Sicily and then was when things started to go into a decline.

—Veronica Hughes Di Grigoli, Author and Sicily Blogger

THIRTEEN

Death, oh yes, it existed of course, but it was something that happened to others.

—Giuseppe Tomasi di Lampedusa

Death in my old neighborhood likely meant an old person had passed. A natural occurrence without a great deal of noisy grieving. The neighborhood people attended as much to drink coffee, eat pastry, and see one another as to honor the recently departed soul. The associated smells, a blend of coffee, confectionery sugar, and carnations, evoke closeness, community, family, and one of the more outward expressions of the fact that we were different from those who lived around us.

Our wakes were crowded and noisy. This is how we escorted our people to the other side. Anything less than, or other than that would have been considered barbaric.

With the death of a younger person, the grief might override the social aspects of the event. A crime-related death (not altogether unexpected) was more solemn and quiet. There was some resignation to mob wakes, a mixed and muffled message of strength and sorrow that meant to say, "This goes with the territory."

Yet an unexpected death by illness or accident was mourned as passionately as in a Puccini opera, especially if the departed soul was a breadwinner. The volume of a widow's shrieks was in an inverse relationship to how well taken-care of she would be in her widowhood.

Those left-behind wives felt an abject terror of facing a life of increasing struggles alone. Our upstairs neighbor Carmeline, a woman widowed young, worked as a waitress the rest of her days after her husband's accidental death. More than once I heard her say to my mother, "Money does not buy happiness, Helen, but it sure makes the sorrows a whole lot easier to bear."

Carmeline was sending my mother a message: She should be grateful to have a man at home bringing in a paycheck. Carmeline viewed us as prosperous. Never, at any time in the lives of my parents, did I experience a sense that they were on a stable economic footing. Even late in their lives when they were more or less well-off, my parents behaved as if they were penniless.

FOURTEEN

Aphrodite is beautiful and represents beauty, but her beauty is only a means to an end. The end seems to be desire and sexual intoxication; actually, it is fertility.

—Erich Neumann, Amor and Psyche

Sicily does not belong to anybody, but we belong to her.

—Michela Musolino, Sicilian-American Folksinger

It is all part of this magical place. When I look at this nature, I am subconsciously aware of the history of the island, and that it has been conquered by bandits, marauders, and so many different people. The one thing that they can't take away from them is nature. This island is beautiful, period.

—Karen La Rosa, Sicily Aficionada

When the sun is out in Sicily, Sicilians are out of doors. Sicilians live the greater part of their lives outside. They seem nearly always to be in the street interacting with one another.

On the grounds of the Norman Palace in old Palermo, a group of grandfatherly-looking men has moved a heavy wooden table under one of the more sheltering shade trees.

There they are, fifteen or twenty of them, playing cards, smoking, and arguing. Occasionally a huge burst of laughter will rise from them. Then they settle down again to a moderately loud noise level. This is what most Sicilians do. They gather together. They connect based on proximity, their idle time, and their "Sicilian-ness."

For some reason, Sicily has been kept unspoiled. Let's start from number one, a life outside. A life that's healthy. The outdoors, having been brought up there, you do not realize till you go out of Sicily and you remember all this time spent outside. When I was little I was always outside. My town was a small paradise. We would be outside all the day. So everything is outside. I remember then, even the sauce, the dry sauce was left outside to dry making things so tasty. I was thinking that in Brussels...oh my god, I miss my country so much. The smell of the zagara. This is the flower of the lemon. If you go into the garden where I grew up...I do not know. It is something I cannot describe—is gelsi (the mulberry blossom). It is something in May that comes up. You climb the trees. You have the smell, it is not reproducible. It is the smell of the oil on warm bread...like salt and anchovies. It is not reproducible. It is something you will have in your brain forever. No matter how many films you do. No matter how many papers you write, no matter how high a quality a picture is, you have high fidelity, high HD, now, whatever... The one thing that you cannot reproduce is the smell of your country. I am actually waiting again or perhaps when I retire to start my life outside. Or change for a job being outside in Sicily.

—Giovanni Morreale, Engineer and Editor, Times of Sicily

Near a room I take in Trapani, a pair who appear to be mother and son operate a tiny sandwich shop facing the waterfront with hardly room enough inside for the tiny oven and coolers. Outside the front door, though, there were many tables and chairs right up to the sidewalk.

When I arrive in Trapani, the proprietress of my room is nowhere to be found. So I decide to lunch at the neighboring sandwich shop. In Sicily, you learn to use your waiting time well because, in Sicily, you have to wait often. The son takes my order. The mother prepares my modest and delicious lunch of a salami panino on crusty bread and a cold drink.

For the rest of my stay, the mother, who often holds court at an outside table, greets me as I walk to or from my room. In the evening, after their tiny rush of business for the evening meal, mother and son sit outdoors. They speak to passing neighbors and friends and family members arriving on foot or by Vespa. Everyone sits outside. They talk, laugh, and play cards late into the night, all seeming to enjoy one another's company. They do this every night.

Each person in that gathering could have done something else. I'm sure the young ones had video games or could go someplace to hang out with friends their own ages. Yet they arrive there every night and it sounds as if they're enjoying themselves. It sounds like love to me.

Back in Palermo, Giuseppe the innkeeper is normally one of the kindest human beings I have known in my life, until this morning. After my second Italian lesson, he refuses to engage any further in English communications with me.

An English-style pub is within walking distance from Giuseppe's. It is as English as anything can be in Sicily. They serve a variety of beers yet the food remains Sicilian. For happy-hour, a decidedly American phenomenon, they serve antipasto for the price of a beer. They do this until eight in the evening. When I'm on my own, I have one beer and take my evening meal from the antipasto table.

My waiter speaks very good English. He has been to the States and wants to move there to live in Santa Monica or West Hollywood. The America he longs for is the one I long to escape. However, I have some prosperity. He is young, well-educated, and works as a waiter because it is the only job available to him. He has a young man's dreams.

From time to time, I wonder to myself if there can ever be a genuinely thriving economy in Sicily. All of these people eat, smoke, and have sex. They yell and scream at the television during futbol matches. They complain about the Church yet remain Catholic. Many community events are also religious events. They participate while simultaneously complaining about them.

And everywhere I look I see so many suffering Madonnas and bleeding Jesuses. These are the images for life. No wonder Sicilians are such romancers. Romantic love is among their meager opportunities to transcend a religiously imposed pessimism.

For breakfast, Giuseppe has fresh fruit and his near-amphetamine Café Nero. I remember the flavor of Sicilian strawberries and North African bananas from my childhood. Unlike most fruit in America now, fruit in Sicily tastes like it should.

Fruit, bread, and coffee are the Sicilian drugs of choice. Everyone is on a sugar high. And the Sicilian sugar high seems to make more junkies than drunks.

I walk Via San Augustino up to the market at Cappo Santa Anna. I find two puppet repair shops. Both are closed.

I really want to go inside.

I also find a starker Palermo. There are no well-scrubbed kids on these streets. Many young men have sunken cheeks that indicate the AIDS cocktail, more likely a result from needle sharing than sex. It's a very rough part of town.

Nearly every young man has a girlfriend. Even obviously gay boys accompany heavier or less pretty girls. A guy of maybe seventeen––diminutive, dressed more extravagantly than most—hugs and kisses all of his best girl buddies at the front door of Feltrinelli, a book and record store with great classical and jazz collections. They and others are gathered in front of the store watching a group of hip-hop dancers. The young performers are dazzling—as good as any I've seen anywhere. Their skills and energy levels are staggering.

On Sunday, I search nearly an hour for the Museum of Contemporary Art. I unwittingly pass it several times. The building has no clear signage nor a posted address. Inside the Museum are more employees than art lovers, which seems strange to me. On a Sunday afternoon in most big cities, such a museum would be bustling.

The collection here is almost entirely Sicilian or Sicily-related. The neoclassical of the late Nineteenth Century is almost comical in its anachronism. Most of the paintings show no signs of the influences that were going on throughout the rest of Europe at the time of their creation.

With the Sicilian super-painter Renato Gattuso, and the Group of Four (including painter Lia Pasqualino Noto and sculptors Giovanni Barbera and Nino Franchina), I begin to see something that is truly modern and entirely Sicilian. These artists were forthrightly opposed to the dominant Novecento movement and the rise of Fascism in their time.

A young contemporary painter, Alesandro Bazat, captures a present-day Palermo in fast brush strokes and almost obnoxious colors. These paintings exude a palpable anger that could very easily have slipped into a mythic nostalgia reminiscent of Thomas Hart Benton. His work has a very American scent.

The North Africans, for example, taught the Sicilians how to make ceramics. They developed that into Majolica pottery, which every-body knows is Italian. They do not know it came from Sicily.

—Veronica Hughes Di Grigoli, Author and Sicily Blogger

Ceramics from Erice, a mountain town on the far western point of Sicily, have their own style and history and are not a recent creation, but date back many centuries. Findings confirm that even in Greek and Roman times and before the time of Christ, there were kilns here in Erice. What gives value to ceramics is the work. From craftsmanship to utility, shape, and especially decoration, what actually makes an object valuable is the decoration.

Nothing compares to the fourth-century mosaics unearthed at the Villa Casale near Piazza Armerina.

At the very beginning of the European tradition, Antonello da Messina, a very great and very important artist, because although he came from Sicily, from Messina specifically, he was also the man who acted as the intermediary between Flemish art and Venetian art.

—Joseph Farrell, Author and Sicilian Scholar

Antonello will be the great hinge, the transition between medieval painting and Renaissance painting both in Sicily and in Naples. The

Annunciation comes from this land because the objects represented within are from this territory. He documents the sacred or the symbolic theme of the sacred dropped into the reality of where the artist lives. It was not by chance that Leonardo placed the Annunciation in a garden, in a landscape, because the landscape is not nature described as an object but it is the world, the creation of God.

—Michele Romano

The museum has a cafeteria with a chef. When I enter, the handsome young manager is seated with his young, beautiful assistant. They are sharing a meal and they are the only persons seated in the dining room. When I arrive in search of a cold drink, the pretty assistant jumps up. The handsome manager continues eating.

Countries in Europe, Sicily included, with any aspiration smell too much of the United States for my liking. Regardless of what the young people may say about the U.S., their tastes are decidedly American.

I have a panini for dinner outside at a sandwich shop called Bacco. The place is packed. The proprietor brings the television outside for his patrons: Naples versus Juventus. I am the only one alone at a table. The rest are crowded together drinking beer and completely rapt by the game. I am completely rapt by the utter madness that defines sports in Sicily. It's the same as it was in Kansas City throughout my childhood. Why am I surprised?

The Sunday evening passeggiata (stroll) along Via Maqueda and at Politeama ends promptly at 8 p.m. almost as if someone blows a whistle. Soon motorcycles and Vespas are shooting stars down the boulevards. The young have taken over the night.

One of the most traditional art forms of Sicily is the Puppet Theater, a unique combination of what might be called a poor man's opera and a hockey game.

Fiorenzo Napoli, a Traditional Sicilian Puppeteer, learned the art form of the puppeteer communicating from him to the puppet and from the puppet to the audience, and here is where the alchemy or the magic of puppeteering happens. Sicilians know these stories very well. It is the righteous hero versus the traitorous, vile bad guy. Audiences have been known to get so involved in these performances that fist fights break out.

Domenico DiMauro, a traditional Sicilian Cart Painter is one hundred and two years old. His talent was recognized at an early age and since then he has been awarded nearly every tribute achievable by a man in his craft. Looking back on his career, he notes, "I've been a painter for more than eighty years. I started when I was twelve years old and by the age of fourteen. I was painting in the province of Messina."

"I still paint, because I love painting. In fact, I finished a painting just a little while ago. When someone begins a job, they must do it with passion otherwise it is worth nothing. That's how it is."

Traditional Sicilian painted donkey cart

FIFTEEN

Nowhere do we more stubbornly encounter the reality of soul—in itself such a dim and wispy idea—than in the crosspatch nastiness of bad tempers, the insights that slip away, the sensitive vanities that will not be mollified.

—James Hillman, Anima

Perhaps my regret for having never been a son plays a large role in my emotional indifference.

—Fernando Pessoa, The Book of Disquiet

Throughout my research and interviews, I've found many scientific and decidedly non-scientific claims about the powers of Mt. Etna, Sicily's iconic volcano. I especially enjoy the comments of the great modern chronicler of Sicilian history, Denis Mack Smith. He has written,

Witchcraft, bigamy, and sexual perversion seem to have been the most frequent offenses which came before these courts. Perhaps Sicilians had become accustomed to the more lax traditions of the Greeks and Arabs. Homosexuality, for example, which particularly offended the government, was apparently rife: Charles V persuaded himself that it caused the frequent earthquakes that plagued Sicily.

Smith goes on to tell us, "The chief hangman of Palermo,

who carried out some of these executions for homosexuality, was himself executed for the same offense in 1608."

At the time we were shooting the film, we had scheduled an interview with Denis Mack Smith who was, then, ninety-five. While in London, his daughter notified us that he had suffered a mild heart attack and that an interview was not advisable at that time. We could not return to London, so we had to give up on that interview. Smith lived two more years, dying at age ninety-seven.

We are in a place where there are three continents that face each other. We have Africa a short distance from here. We are the extreme of Europe, but we are part of Europe. We have Asia to the other side.

— Carmelo Giafriddu, Geologist and Etna Expert

While we've been working on the film, Etna has had a series of remarkable eruptions. And you can see from space that the tectonic plates of Africa and Asia are close by, and that collision is creating those eruptions.

Etna, in a way, represents the best and to a certain extent, the worst of Sicily. It dominates the island. It gives the abundance to the island, but it is also the destroyer.

—Andrew Edwards, Author and Scholar

We live around the highest active volcano in Europe, one of the most active volcanoes in the world. In Sicilian, a place like this where recent lava flow flew down, is called sciara. That is a word that comes from Arabic, and it is the same etymological root of the desert of Northern Africa, Sahara. This part of the road, it was

*spared by the lava flow. But look where the lava flow was, like
around there were hotels, ski lifts, restaurants, the same day all the
eruption, everything got destroyed. We have a special place where
forces of nature work and where you can see the beauty in the
force of nature. We have not only explosions and lava flow. This is
a place where we have a high potentiality of major earthquakes.*
— Carmelo Giafriddu

SIXTEEN

Food is emblematic of 'Love and Strife'.
With so many outside influences and so unusual a combination of
ingredients, Sicilian food is unique. There is a dark dimension to
food in Sicily based on the excesses of a few at the expense
of others who were malnourished.

—Arthur Stanley Riggs, Vistas of Sicily

Food is a wonderful and fascinating part of Sicilian life. There are
a great many contributing factors. Well, it is precarious having
volcanoes all around, but what volcanoes do is provide the most
fertile soil there is.

 —Mark Spano, Filmmaker and Author

Sicily, it seems very likely, is the place where pasta first entered Italian
culture and the Italian economy, dried durum wheat pasta. The Ital-
ians invented the fork almost certainly to eat macaroni with.

 —John Dickie, Author and Scholar

This is Nonna Vicenza, my mother, the beginner of our history.
Eighteen years ago, Nonna Vicenza begin this place with my
father, my sister, and our family. All of our products are based
on old Sicilian recipes with the main ingredients being almonds,

pistachios, hazelnuts, walnuts, but above all, almonds and pista-chios. Sicilian sweets have many cultural layers from the Arabs, the Romans, the Normans, and the more they had, the more they contributed. This is molded in these forms and then the ricotta is added. This is the sponge cake to which the ricotta and the choco-late drops will be added. In my house, you could always smell the sweets because my mother made them for friends. The sweets must be made with quality ingredients. The people must feel like they are part of the family.

—Paolo Pistone, Proprietor of Nonna Vicenza, a Sicilian bakery

When I think about food, I always have to go back to my fami-ly because family is where you are initiated to food. Food is not about nourishing you from the physical point of view. It is about nourishing your soul. It is about love. Sicilians wanted to devel-op whatever the Greeks, the Romans, the Arabs have left us into something great and magnificent.

—Katia Amore, Magazine Editor and Teacher

Italian food is city food essentially because cities have been the motors of Italian food civilization since the Middle Ages. There's a whole set of interlocking reasons to do with social status, to do with commerce, to do with the local pride, that generates this strong sense of identification with food over the centuries. There's also an investment of social identity, if you like. Good manners, very, very important. That's to do with rules of behavior, saying, I am not a peasant. I am not one of those foreigners. I am part of this culture.

—John Dickie, Author and Scholar

We went early one morning to Mr. Brancato's just outside of Catania where he and his grandsons make the traditional Sicilian ricotta. Sicily aficionada Karen La Rosa describes sampling Signor Brancato's cheese as "a religious experience."

Sicilians are as finicky and as exacting about olive oil as they are about wine. Near Aci Castello, the Nicolosi family grow their own olives and make their own olive oil. This is not a commercial venture. They do this for their family and their friends.

It is often assumed that Italian food somehow is a peasant food. That's a terrible insult to the enormous sufferings of the Italian peasantry over the millennia. The reality was hunger, if you were lucky.

—John Dickie, Author and Scholar

People were so poor. Families were desperate to survive. When a child was turned over and became a caruso and entered into this, the dead loan, you were either extremely impoverished or you were profiting from this system. The idea was that you were beginning your life as a miner. You were beginning your life as a working adult to support the family. These children were essentially turned over to these miners. They were also subjected to a lot of sexual assaults and abuse by the miners that they worked under. There was a code of honor. The survival of the family came first. Although there's a definite sense of pride and legacy that surrounds a mining community in Sicily, a lot of the history is not taught. People wanted to forget.

—Olivia Kate Cerrone, Author and Writing Instructor

I awaken before everyone at the palazzo. Giuseppe has provided me with coffee and gone off to the bakery for today's bread and pastries. A young workman walks through the sunroom where I am writing. He glares at me as my head comes up from my notebook to see him pass. He takes me for God-knows-what without attempting to speak. The fear of the unknown.

Dinner last night was interesting. The food was good despite the fact that some tourists had found the place. The restaurant staff was very put-off by Carlus and me, maybe because we didn't eat a full menu. Or maybe our couplehood was off-putting to them.

In most places, Carlus and I do not call much attention to ourselves. Maybe because of our age difference people don't assume we're a couple. But Sicilians can smell sex, even homosexual sex. This place is charged with male-male eroticism. I'm not certain I could live here. So many encounters, so sexually charged, would continually interrupt my focus. I would get nothing done.

It's raining this morning. No Sicilian sun today. It's chilly on Giuseppe's sunporch. He has just returned from the bakery with breakfast. For the rest of the morning, I talk to him about Sicily and the world. Carlus and I have come to love him in the short time we have all three spent together.

Last night, there was a gay pride event in Palermo. It was a rather meager event by United States standards. Not many people turned out other than the younger kids (who would go anywhere to hear a free band). It was important, though. Mr. Gay Europe is an Italian young man. Very handsome. He called his whole family to the stage. It was very touching.

The wedding in Monreale was also very touching. How did I get so sentimental in my old age? The actual major crisis of my life has been exclusion.

Why do I talk so much to these people? I should share less and put that energy into my journal. It's simply habit. My journalizing is so broad. I am more than capable of writing in greater detail. I want to write as if I'm taking morphine—very slowly and meticulously, like a mosaic. I understand why Sherlock Holmes smoked opium. It opened him to the most minute detail. I'll stop now.

This evening I walk the passeggiata. The young people are so beautiful. I love them. They are out with their friends, laughing. They seem to love each other more than American youth. (Maybe I imagine this.) Their affection seems much more authentic.

There are more gay kids than first meets the eye. And they are with their "girlfriends."

As I walk alone on Via Magueda, a man on a motorcycle pulls up to the curb head-on as I walk toward him. He makes no eye contact with me. I have no idea that his stop has anything to do with me until it happens again later in the evening. I am certain these encounters would not have been of a merely conversational nature had I taken up either of them. I can't find an open music venue or an open gay bar. I'm in bed by 11:30.

This is as good a place as any to discuss narcissism. James Hillman has written, "Modern man has an accumulated debt to Aphrodite on which she is today exacting payments at a furious rate. It is as if she were actually demanding souls for all the centuries they were denied her by Judeo-Christian repression." From this repression, we are smothering.

What most us think of as narcissism is actually something of a breathing apparatus for the otherwise suffocating. These are individuals who have had their life's breath so forcibly squeezed from them that they take any and all opportunities to grab a breath simply to know that they are alive and capable of breathing. Creativity may come of this gasping.

I write of this because so many people I meet in Sicily could be written off as narcissists. Unless we view these individuals in the light of millennia of inescapable setbacks, we will not be able to find compassion and understanding.

Each of us could point to the various narcissists we love because, or in spite of, their breathing problems. They are human bonsais contorted so early in their days that they hardly understand what has been done to them.

Pain and anger of any type require compassion and care for our breathless friends. Fortunately, there's air aplenty for the breathing and space aplenty for the stretching and growing if they'll just take advantage of it.

Such observations, plus familiarity with death and its mysteries, will free our narcissistic friends from their constricted existences.

The invention of ghosts is wishful thinking on our part. It allows us to deal with the irreversibility of death. We cannot get influential friends or the smart or the rich to fix this one for us.

SEVENTEEN

...opera is less complete than vaudeville, which at least inaugurates the comedy of an exhaustive enumeration.

—Samuel Beckett, Proust

In Sicily, young men don't seem as lacking in simple kindness as the Sicilian toughs from the neighborhood where I grew up. They were a cruel lot to their peers, to their girlfriends, and often to their own families. Even the yelping peddlers in the open markets of Palermo, brimming with that special brand of vitality manifest only by a particular combination of Sicilian-ness and testosterone, seem much more good-natured in ways I seldom saw in the young men from my upbringing.

Was good humor lost in crossing the Atlantic?

Young people seem to be everywhere in Sicily, they don't have jobs. They all look great. Even the rare ones without the natural beauty given to most Sicilians seem quite fashionable. Even a pimpled twelve-year-old has a fabulous coiff.

Young Sicilian men are more naturally friendly than the young women. In Sicily, a young woman's eyes do not dare to wander. Even so much as the slightest eye-contact with a male of any age thrusts a girl of any age into open season for sexual advances.

Sicilian women rarely grow as tall as the thin, statuesque beauties you encounter in Rome or the northern Italian regions. Sicilian women are shorter and tend to have more hips than breasts, "Women as God intended them to be," my friend Alberto says. "Men who want women without hips are really gay and don't know it."

I laugh heartily at this comment.

Most Sicilians have dark complexions and dark hair, but certainly not all. I was amazed by how many fair-skinned blue- and green-eyed Sicilians I met. Then there are the most intriguing of combinations of light eyes and dark complexion. This has an enchantment all its own—one I find nearly irresistible.

The real mystery of Sicily surrounds the haves and have-nots. It involves appearance, impersonation, or usurpation. Oftentimes, it is more important to appear to be something than to be the thing itself.

Sicilians love fashion that is larger than life. This is the grandeur that can only be realized by those who have been left out. The poor here manage to play the role of boss but they have little imagination for the social roles of a modern economy.

Today, in Sicily, youth are royalty. This is why Sicilian weddings are such Trimalchian feasts. Even the poorest families will spend two years' wages on a wedding. These weddings are more like coronations that nuptials. They are a day in the sun for the happy couple. Post-coronation, the coach turns back into a pumpkin and, in many cases, the bride and groom turn into struggling adults.

Sicilians should not live in high-rises. They need the earth, the sky, and the sea. Tall buildings are for people of a written poetic tradition who live in their heads. Sicilians have remained in an oral poetic tradition. They need the elements, animals, and one another. High-rises are for making profits, not for Sicilians to live in. This is as true in the United States as it is in Sicily. Yet populations emigrating to the western democracies get stacked almost immediately into tall buildings.

In the downtown Kansas City of my childhood, a number of our co-inhabitants came up from Arkansas, Oklahoma, and the Ozarks. Blacks and whites. They had never lived in tall buildings. Mexicans and Sicilians from essentially farming villages came for jobs and got stacked. Most of them never adapted. Ask a policeman in Palermo, or Durham, North Carolina, or Kansas City, Missouri. "Stacked" does not work for every kind of people.

New Yorkers are better stacked than most. New Yorkers are all about what someone else has made—the latest play, the best new restaurant, the most promising IPO. Those who want and need to make things themselves need to be on the ground.

I have never been to Hong Kong, but from my reading I've gleaned that it may be the capital of the most successful stacking of people. But for most of Sicily? NO!

In Sicily, I play the comic foreigner, the neophyte—a role Sicilians have perfected. They love it. I reflect themselves back to them. I actively engage in seeming adorable. Sicilians love adorable. I've known this since I was two years old.

EIGHTEEN

How strange that I should be called a destitute woman!
When I have all of these treasures locked in my heart.

—Blanche DuBois, "A Streetcar Named Desire"
by Tennessee Williams

In Sicily, compassion is not felt, it is manifest. Everything is manifest. Sicilians know well that what you hold privately in your heart is a lie and that death is standing at our left shoulders ready to tap us at any time. Knowledge of death's impending tap despoils the heart's treasures.

To Sicilians, what we share is who we are. What is held back represents our contempt for life, an allegation made to the world that we are owed something.

Harsh limitations imposed on Sicilians who left the island were sometimes carried with them to the New World. In the United States, my family didn't know what was around the corner from them, metaphorically speaking. They held onto the habits of the "Old Country."

There's a story from when Italy was unified in 1861. Among the first laws passed was mandatory education of children so that children had to go to school. But in Sicily, there were no roads for them to get to school.

—Massimo Lo Schiavo, Mayor of Santa Maria di Salina

People that work in the public administration are highly union-ized. They've got their ways of working, and there's no incentive to change. Without a judiciary system that functions, we will not attract the big investments. We have probably more Sicilian people living outside of Sicily than people living in Sicily.

—Nino Casimo, Engineer and Mayor of Basicò

The regulations are always the same. So muddled that even those coming from the European community become obstacles to economic development. There are too many levels of law, too many regulations that cannot be reconciled. This becomes really difficult for entrepreneurs. Today I am saying to my young people go abroad, develop yourselves, and come back a few years later, because unfortunately, what we have isn't enough.

—Massimo Lo Schiavo

They will ask you favors, they will ask you to hire the people that they will indicate to you. If you want to build something here, you need a permit. And if you want a permit, you will ask the politicians and the politician will ask you money.

—Giovanni Gallo, University Professor

The degree of brain drain from Sicily is terrifying. It is a real shame that Sicily, in every generation, loses the brightest, the most motivated, the most talented because nepotism stops them finding opportunities in Sicily, so they go abroad and they are outstanding, they are spectacular. But in Sicily, they're prevented from achieving their potential.

—Veronica Hughes Di Grigoli, Author and Sicily Blogger

Mosaicoon is a startup that was born in Sicily. Like the standard in tech company, we were born in our garage. What we created is a new unique model for creation, production, distribution, and monitoring of video line. We have a very huge potential in this country. We work for some of the biggest company. We're wide. We were the first company with venture capital found in the south of Italy. When I started to make things happen, they started thinking so probably we can invest in this company. Being in Sicily is not a limit. For me, obviously, it is way better than to live in Milan, to live in London.

—Ugo Parodi, co-CEO of Mosaicoon

Entry to the Market of Vucciria in Palermo

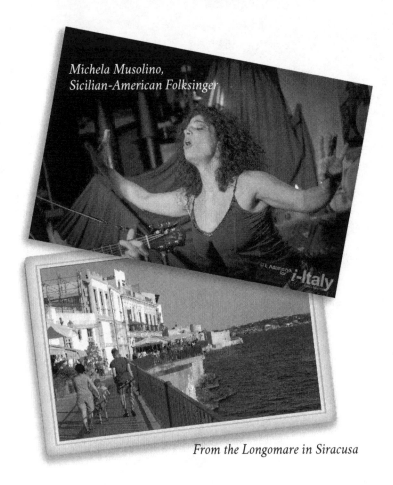

Michela Musolino,
Sicilian-American Folksinger

From the Longomare in Siracusa

NINETEEN

Italian Catholicism, I am happy to say, retains the most florid pictorialism, the bequest a pagan past that was never lost.

—Camille Paglia, Sexual Personae

The fact that the Sicilian land could rumble under your feet, the land itself could rain fire down on you makes Sicilians a little bit edgy about what's around the corner.

In 1693, there was a terrible earthquake. Actually, it happened in two shocks. The first happened on January 9th. The one that did more damage happened on January 11th, and it caused massive destruction in the southeastern corner of Sicily, the part that is known as the Val di Noto. Individual builders and contractors within those cities and towns were given a great deal of freedom and power to proceed with the reconstruction that was sorely needed. It was actually a blessing because it allowed for the proliferation known as the Baroque. There wasn't one overarching plan. There was a kind of design language, a grammar that everyone had to follow. They used these designs in a way that adapted to local conditions.

—Thomas Puleo, Author and Scholar

When a great disaster happens, as terrible as it is, as much tragedy as it causes, it also allows for a capacity for change in that particular society that was there inside the hearts and minds of the people but was being held back because of the old infrastructure, because of the old institutional ways. All of a sudden, when those old curvy, medieval streets are destroyed and then eventually replaced with a very rational grid pattern that was characteristic of the Baroque, there was a great physical and psychological opening in society. You look at a Baroque building. There is a personality, a character, a liveliness, a movement to Baroque buildings. Baroque buildings are alive, and Sicilian Baroque buildings are the most alive of all. Baroque is all about mixing and harmonizing various elements, and of course this is the entire history of Sicily, right, is this need to constantly harmonize the mix of influences that have been at the heart of its identity and its daily experience for millennia.

—Thomas Puleo, Author and Scholar

Palazzo Biscari, a baroque villa in Catania, is a prime example of the Sicilian love of decorative excess. The current resident, Ruggero Moncada Paternò Castello, is a descendant of the original owner. He describes a bit of its history this way.

The first man of this family arrived in Sicily in 1053. Paterno is the name of the family. This is Palazzo Biscari, and we have lived in this building for 11 generations. Within the building we have 600 rooms. It was not enough, so he bought another (property) near the building and gave to (his)lover. A building of another 200 rooms. This ballroom is like a guitar, so the music come down like in a guitar. Ignacio, Vincent, Ignacio, Vincent. From Robert to Vincent, the grandfather of my grandmother was Robert. My grandmother, Yolanda, my father, me, and after us, my two daughters.

TWENTY

Sicily has always been rather finicky about its saints.
—Arthur Stanley Riggs from Vistas of Sicily

Sicily has been and remains a land of incoming immigrants. It has also been a land that sends immigrants from its shores. These cultural shifts have not always been easy. These same cultural shifts are the principle source of Love and Strife throughout the island's history. Yet, if beauty is the promise of Love for Sicilians; then, the island's blended culture is the promise fulfilled, a fulfillment that is uniquely its own and shared by all. From their three-sided island, Sicilians enjoy an abundant and diverse culture, earned through three millennia of Strife now offered to the world with well-earned Love.

Reading gave me an understanding of the cultural importance of Sicily and the world's ignorance of it. Most Sicilians do not even know the importance of their region, which has been treated by the north for so long like a leper colony. If Sicily is a leper colony, northerners helped to create it. There is much greatness in Sicily. And it can be tapped.

As I have written earlier, Sicilians are not tough guys. They are a gentle people. This gentility has emboldened invaders, so-called nobility or grandees, the church and the Mafia to push them around, to steal everything of any value on their island, even to rape Palermo of architectural treasures and replace them with high-rise apartments that were slums before anyone had even moved into them. If anyone moved into them.

Hundreds of apartment buildings stand vacant all over Palermo—actually all over the island. The Mafia hates Sicily—the rape of Palermo. The high-rises of Bagheria—the junk that was built and unmentioned—suggest self-loathing. Violating the land and sea is as grievous as violating your own mother or child. Same for gambling, prostitution, and drugs. These aren't simply lifestyle choices. These activities have massive consequences that affect everyone. Putting a knife in any Sicilian is putting a knife in Sicily.

Different cultures, centuries of different culture that's what makes Palermo so fascinating. In New York or Chicago, the crime rate is 50 times higher than here but nobody says, oh, Chicago, crime or Mafia or whatever. More than 30 years ago, I came here to Palermo. For a moment I thought they were shooting a film about Beirut or something like that. It gave the impression that the war had ended the day before. Our street was a bomb site in the real sense of the word as the American bombs had left it in 1943. And this area was in (a) terrible condition. So it was a very difficult town to live in. Our idea is to maintain the memory of Giuseppe Tomasi di Lampedusa who spent here the last year or so of his life. That library has remained exactly as it was when he died. It was also the only room of the house that he managed to furnish in a nice way with whatever he had salvaged from the ruins of his palazzo, which had been razed to the ground by the American bombs in April '43. So we try to keep his memory alive as much as possible.

—Nicoletta Polo, Palermitana and Guardian of Lampedusa Legacy

He started around '52 planning something. The first book of the Italian Sicilian was "The Leopard", and it is a book about life and death. It is a book, too, that explains what kind of expectation you must have in life for your happiness. The professor of philosophy at Palermo University was a Catholic. Cardolella said that this was the most obscene book that had been written since the times of de Sade. Apart from that, though, the readers liked it very much.

—Gioacchino Lanza Tomasi, Impresario and Guardian of
   Lampedusa Legacy

My friend Luca in Siracusa asks me what I think of the news that some Italian futbol matches had been fixed. I said I live in America where many of the elections were fixed. I was much more concerned with corrupt democracy than corrupted business. If democracy is fair, corrupt businesses will face the consequences. Then we talk for a long time about the subprime mortgage rackets. I won't call it a crisis. A hurricane is a crisis.

How dare any Anglo-Saxon American point a finger at Sicilians?

Luca laughs about friends who pay five hundred Euros for shoes and whine when they get scratched. Who wears five-hundred Euro shoes? he asks. The parents of girlfriend's don't think he dresses nicely enough. Luca wears what Americans call "dress casual."

I am inclined to believe that Luca's family is considerably more prosperous than his girlfriend's. Yet they want him to look like the prize that he is. How else will their friends know that their daughter has made a good match? This is terribly important to them. It was to my friends, too. You must look the part.

Luca asks me why American houses are so easy to break into. If you had a villa at the beach, Luca says, and it didn't have walls and barbed wire and broken glass stuck into the concrete someone would come to visit while you were gone and take all your valuables. In Sicily it could be everything— dishes, towels, toilet paper, everything. No thief worth the title would take such things in the United States

Teresa, another Siracusan friend, had an American physician son-in-law who had taken her daughter off to frozen Vermont to live. Teresa said she would only visit in the summer. She also found it astounding that her doctor son-in- law would come home from a day spent "doctoring," change from a suit to blue-jeans, and go outside to till his own land or to take down trees.

"Why," she asked me, "would anyone do such things if he did not have to? He is a doctor. It doesn't seem proper."

CONCLUSION

And anyone who has once known this land can never be quite free from the nostalgia for it.

—D. H. Lawrence, from Sea and Sardinia

Reimagine Sicily. Reimagine it with me. Reimagining 3,000 years of culture and beauty and tradition that are not completely European. They're not completely Middle Eastern. They're not completely Asian or North African, but they have the flavor of all of those. That is why Sicily is so different and why I am so dazzled by the place and the people. Come with me, let me take you to a place that you've only heard about. You have no idea what a remarkable place it is. I will show you.

The most frequent question to me that I receive so frequently, especially here in Italy and in Sicily, why did you come back? Whatever I might do, I am kind of helping and I am doing my part. Come here and live the community that we have and help to improve it.

—Shoan Knopp, Repatriated Sicilian-American and Teacher

This is the Sicily we found. Whatever people may think about Sicily, it is time to reimagine it.

ABOUT THE AUTHOR

Writer and filmmaker Mark Spano is promoting his recent novel "Midland Club" which he recently adapted for the screen. He is presently in development for *Midland Club* the film. He has also completed a book entitled *Kidding the Moon*. Spano resides in rural Orange County, North Carolina with his partner, a dog, and one chicken that no longer lays eggs.

www.thunderpress.com
www.sicilymovie.com